LAE

VILLAGE AND CITY

PUBLISHED WITH THE ASSISTANCE OF A GRANT FROM THE

PAPUA NEW GUINEA UNIVERSITY OF TECHNOLOGY

LAE

VILLAGE AND CITY

IAN WILLIS

MELBOURNE UNIVERSITY PRESS
1974

First Published 1974

Printed in Australia by
Wilke and Co. Ltd., Clayton, Victoria 3168 for
Melbourne University Press, Carlton, Victoria 3053
U.S.A. and Canada: ISBS Inc., Portland, Oregon 97208
Great Britain, Europe, Middle East, Africa and the Caribbean:
International Book Distributors Ltd, 66 Wood Lane End,
Hemel Hempstead, Hertfordshire HP2 4RG, England

National Library of Australia
Cataloguing in Publication data

Willis, Ian, 1937—
    Lae,village and city/ [by] Ian Willis.—
    Carlton Vic.: Melbourne University Press, 1974.
    Index.
    Bibliography.
    ISBN 0 522 84076 0.
    1. Lae, Papua New Guinea–History. I. Title.
    995

NOTE ON NAMES

The spelling of many New Guinean personal and place names has not been standardized, and sometimes the standardized version is not accurate. For example, many New Guinean names begin with 'ng', which Europeans find difficult to pronounce and usually render simply as 'n'; thus the personal name Ngasingom, which is common in the Lae area, is often written and pronounced 'Nasinom' by Europeans. The rule followed in this book is to use the spelling favoured by the villagers, which is usually phonetic. Thus the largest village near Lae is given its customary village spelling, Butibam, rather than its official spelling 'Butibum'; similarly, rather than 'Kamkumun' that village is spelt Kamkumung, and Lo'wamung is used in preference to the official name, Mount Lunaman.

The use of Christian names was not formerly as common among Germans as among speakers of English. Consequently only the surnames are known of many of the Germans who lived in New Guinea.

ACKNOWLEDGEMENTS

Many people have had a part in the production of this book and without their help it could not have been written. I am particularly indebted to Dr Ian Hogbin of Macquarie University, whose own writings on the Morobe District are essential reading for anyone interested in the problem of cultural change in New Guinea. Dr Hogbin read and provided much valued guidance and criticism of both the manuscript and the thesis from which it grew. Dr Peter Bolger, Hank Nelson and Dr Sione Latukefu of the University of Papua and New Guinea, Professor J. D. Legge of Monash University, also read the original thesis and made many suggestions that proved useful and helpful in writing the book. I am grateful to the Papua New Guinea University of Technology for its grant in aid of publication and to a host of other people who gave me access to records and the benefit of their own knowledge of Lae history. Among them are Dr John Kuder, formerly bishop of the Evangelical Lutheran Church of New Guinea; the Reverend and Mrs Karl Holzknecht of Ampo, Lae; the Reverend G. Schmutterer and the Reverend H. Maurer of Neuendettelsau, West Germany; Madeline Campbell of the Public Solicitor's Office, Port Moresby; Jim Gibbney of the Australian National University; H. E. Seale of Sydney; Adolf Batze of Cairns; Bob Iredale, Alan Roberts, General R. R. McNicoll, Margaret Mustar and the late E. A. ('Pard') Mustar, the late E. W. P. Chinnery, and the late Ian Grabowsky of Melbourne; Horrie Niall, Wan Jin Wah, Wan Kow On, Ela Birrell, Flora Stewart, and Werner Knoll of Lae; and Dr Lawrence Malcolm of Port Moresby, formerly the Regional Health Officer at Lae. I am particularly indebted to Muttu Gware, president of the Butibam Progress Association, Lae, for giving me access to his own records and for arranging interviews with many of the older men and women of Butibam and Kamkumung. Among these village leaders who have given me help have been Cornelius and Moses Ngasengom, Philemon Balob, Kamdering Bukaua, the late Geali Iga, Kahata Wakang, Kising and Mindering Tikandu, Silas Kamake, Karo Ahi, and Steven Ahi, the patron of the Ahi Association. I am grateful to Liz McPhail of Lae for doing my typing quickly, efficiently and carefully, and I am also indebted to my colleague Adrian Boddy for cheerfully doing much of the photography. And finally I wish to acknowledge the encouragement and support I have received from my wife, Margaret, my parents, James and Mavis Willis, and my colleagues, Dr Eric Duncanson, Dr John Sandover, Peter Botsman, Joan Michie and Mary Woodward.

I. W.

Lae
Papua New Guinea
June 1973

CONVERSION FACTORS
(to 3 decimal places)

1 inch	2.54	centimetres
1 foot	0.304	metre
1 mile	1.609	kilometres
1 acre	0.404	hectare
1 pound	0.453	kilogram
1 ton	1.016	tonnes
1 short ton	0.907	tonne

CONTENTS

ILLUSTRATIONS

MAPS

PREFACE

Frantz Fanon, the Negro Algerian nationalist, had much to say about white men who write histories of the colonies in which they live. He believed that

> the settler makes history and is conscious of making it. And because he constantly refers to the history of his mother country, he clearly indicates that he is the extension of that mother country. Thus the history which he writes is not the history of the country which he plunders but the history of his own nation.*

For an Australian living in New Guinea that would be an easy error to make and it is a problem I have had to remember in writing this history. I have been aware of the fact that Lae really has three histories, that of the city, that of the local village community, and that of the contact between city and village; one of my difficulties has been to retain a proper balance between the three. If I have not kept balance and have committed the historiographical sin that Fanon has defined I apologise to the people of the Lae villages and say to them I hope that one day an historian from their number will write their history from their own standpoint.

The writing of this book presented me with a number of other difficulties which became apparent in the text. The first of these was a debilitating lack of reference material covering the field of German and then later Australian administration. Two World Wars and the change-overs between seven separate administrations have ensured that few official records relating to Lae have survived. Similarly there have been difficulties in obtaining oral testimonies, as many of the early residents of Lae have died without leaving records or have dispersed to many corners of the globe. Another problem is that the Lae villagers have never been the subject of a professional linguistic,

* *The Wretched of the Earth*, Penguin, 1967, p. 40

sociological or anthropological investigation, with the result that the historian concerned with Lae lacks many of the aids that are available to historians working in other regions. On the other hand the mission records available to him are rich and varied, covering the entire period of European settlement around Lae. For this reason I have inevitably had to rely heavily on mission sources in lieu of official reference material, oral testimonies and ethnological data. This has given my book an undue bias towards the mission, which I admit, although I would point out that I have endeavoured to maintain perspective.

INTRODUCTION

Papua New Guinea has two cities—Port Moresby, the capital, and Lae—as well as a number of lesser towns such as Rabaul, Madang, Goroka and Mount Hagen. Lae is the country's industrial centre and the headquarters of the Morobe District. It lies at the head of the Huon Gulf, where the coastline turns sharply east along the southern side of the Huon Peninsula after running in a north-westerly direction up the tail of the New Guinea mainland. The dominating feature of this area is the valley of the Markham River, a vast structural trough which is the south-eastern arm of the great Sepik-Ramu-Markham trench.

The Markham, or Busi as local villagers call it, rises in the Finisterre Ranges to the north-west and flows down a broad, flat valley to its mouth two miles west of the city. Although hardly more than one hundred miles long, the river disgorges an immense volume of mud-thickened brown water into the green sea of the Gulf. It is a swift stream swollen by hundreds of tributaries which annually gouge huge quantities of earth from the surrounding mountains. The river is not navigable except by the slender canoes of a few local villagers. There are many sand-bars along the braided length of its course; and there is little settlement on its banks, which in the lower reaches are waterlogged and covered in a dense growth of sago palms and mangrove scrub. In contrast to the monotonous flatness of the valley floor, steep forested mountains sweep up both north and south of the river to peaks of over 10 000 feet. On the eastern side of Lae are two more rivers, the Bumbu and the Busu; these smaller streams flow parallel to the big river but are separated from it by a series of high river terraces across which the city is built. The region is visibly affected by local variations in climate. South-easterly winds bring the coastal strip a heavy rainfall. Lae itself receives 180 inches of rain annually, and its natural vegetation is dense tropical rainforest. In a number of places, however, the soil has been so continually gardened and burnt that broad stretches of *kunai* grass

(*Imperata cylindrica*) have replaced the forest. Inland along the valley the rainfall declines dramatically until areas about twenty miles from the coast receive as little as 40 inches. In such places the rainforest gives way to savannah-like grasslands.

On the outskirts of the city are six traditional villages. One of them, Labu Butu, is effectively isolated from Lae, because it stands amid the Labu Lakes, an extensive series of deltoid lagoons on the far side of the Markham mouth. The other five are all connected to the town by road. Butibam and Ahi-Hengali are the closest to the city. They are contiguous villages built on the eastern bank of the Bumbu a mile from the centre of Lae. Their combined population is about 700. Two miles to their north, and the same distance from Lae, is Kamkumung, a village of 300 inhabitants. The city is expanding so rapidly it seems certain to engulf all three villages within several years. The two remaining villages are more isolated. Wagang, with a population of 270, and Yanga, with 220, are on the beach two and three miles east of Lae respectively. However, the distance by road is about six miles to each and so for the time being they are probably safe from encroachment by the city.

How long the inhabitants of the five villages have lived in the vicinity is uncertain, but it appears they were well established there when Europeans began settling in New Guinea in the late nineteenth century. They are of mixed ancestry. The original occupants were various groupings of Kawa-language speakers who had migrated westward along the coast from the Kawa home area around Bukaua in the centre of the Huon Gulf north coast. They were later joined by groups of migrants known as the Ahi, who spoke a dialect closely related to the present Yalu language of the lower Markham. The Ahi came from the south bank of the Markham near its junction with the Wampit River and had been driven from their home territory by bands of marauding Laewomba-language speakers from the middle Markham. The Ahi scattered before the Laewomba, some fleeing across the Markham to Yalu, others further north into the Saruwaged foothills, some to the Labu villages south of the Markham mouth, and others to the Kawa villages of the north coast. Wherever they went the Ahi were rapidly absorbed. Apparently only at Lae were there sufficient numbers of them to retain a separate identity; but even there assimilation is advanced, and although their descendants now live in a separate village, Ahi-Hengali, they have lost their separate language and have assumed the culture of the Kawa who gave them refuge.

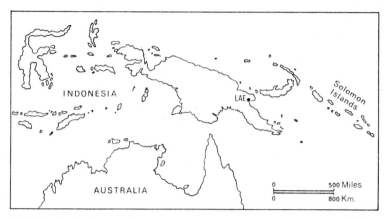

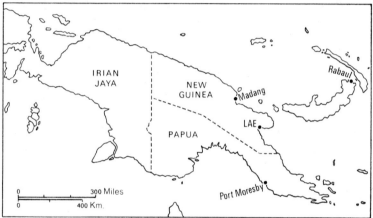

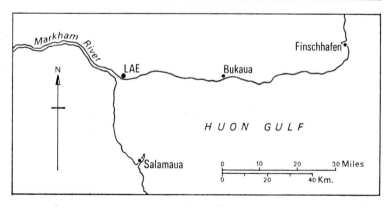

Location of Lae

Villages in the Lae area

Legend:
- Present villages (•)
- Present town boundary (— — —)

Scale: 0 1 2 3 Miles / 0 1 2 3 4 Km.

N

Labels on map:
Busu River
HUON GULF
YANGA
Malahang Road
Plantation
Busu Rd
BUTIBAM
WAGANG VILLAGE
KAMKUMUNG
AHI HENGALI
Butibam Road
Lo'Wamung (Mt Lunaman)
LAE
Markham Road
Bumbu Rd
Bumbu River
Milfordhaven Rd
Air strip
Atzera Range
200 f.
600 f.
1000 f.
Markham River
LABU BUTU
Labu Lakes

The word 'Lae' is derived from the name of the Ahi refugees. Among the Kawa 'Ahi' was pronounced 'Lahi', but through translation into Yabem, the lingua franca spread around the Huon Gulf by the Lutheran Mission early this century, 'Lahi' became first 'Lahe' and then, because the Yabem have trouble in pronouncing 'h', (which does not exist in their language), it became 'Lae'. Similarly, the coastal people referred to the inland groups, both Ahi and Wampar—a group whose ancestral home was on the Watut well upstream from the Markham—collectively, calling them all 'Ahi Wampar'. It is from this expression that the name 'Laewomba' is derived.

Early Europeans visiting the district reserved the word 'Lae' for the people, mistakenly lumping all local groups together under the one name. They referred to the area as Lowamu or Logamu, mispronunciations of the Kawa word *Lo'wamung* ('first hill'). The people used *Lo'wamung* specifically for Mount Lunaman (a later Australian distortion of the Kawa name), the highest point on the river terraces between the Markham and the Bumbu, and the main local landmark. Other early visitors also used the official German name for the hill, Burgberg ('fortress hill'), an appropriate label because when viewed from the sea the hill resembles a huge fort; but by 1914, when the New Guinea colony passed from German to Australian control, 'Lae' was being used generally to describe both the people and the place.

The Lae people at the time of their first contact with the West were a small group of hamlet dwellers dependent on their environment for most of their needs but maintaining trading links with groups further afield to obtain the resources their own area lacked. As elsewhere in Papua New Guinea, many activities were carried out co-operatively, and the members of each of the residential groups were mutually dependent. They thus had need to live at peace with one another, and usually maintained cordial relations with their neighbours. The region was well endowed by nature and no one lived in want. The people preserved a socio-economic balance which enabled them to cope with the vicissitudes of their primitive existence. But they were not prepared for the cataclysm permanent European settlement would create.

Early contacts with the West were spasmodic. The first Europeans to come were French, English and German navigators. They arrived at infrequent intervals but made a deep impression, and the people soon learnt both to fear the white man's guns and desire his material possessions. The explorers were followed by officials of the German colonial administration, and by labour recruiters and missionaries in the late 1880s and 1890s. Each of these agents of European influence made its own peculiar demands: the government officials wanted the people to be compliant, the recruiters wanted them to enlist for long periods of employment away from home, and the missionaries wanted them to abandon their traditional culture in favour of Christianity. The people did not offer much resistance to these various pressures for they stood to benefit by co-operating with Europeans. They hoped to gain Western material wealth and knowledge as well as protection from enemies living in the hinterland.

The contrasting needs of the white men and the villagers created conditions under which the traditional society began changing to accommodate the Western intrusions. With permanent European settlement and the growth of a town at Lae, the transformation of the local society accelerated. When the people began to perceive what was happening to their culture they became less and less willing to accede to the demands of the Europeans. As the process of change gained momentum their resistance became more stubborn, and many of them attempted to turn their backs on the West. That was not possible, however, for European culture had made too many inroads. Instead they had to make a rapprochement with the white men in their midst.

This book charts the course of the adjustments the villagers had to make to absorb the shock of European settlement. It shows how the intrusion of Western culture altered the social fabric of the village community, creating new and severe tensions. At the same time it points to the resilience of local society, which was able to adapt to the pressures of European settlement and to maintain its corporate identity while being forced from the stone age into the twentieth century in the space of less than one hundred years.

I

THE LAE BEFORE CONTACT WITH EUROPEANS

A glance at the map of New Guinea gives several immediate impressions: long coastline, masses of mountains, broad valleys, and the Huon Peninsula pointing like a stubby finger at the arc of islands to the north and east. Movement around the peninsula and along the south coast of the Huon Gulf is restricted to the narrow coastal plain which broadens out only near the mouth of the Markham. The Markham and its tributaries lead into an extensive network of mountain valleys which shelter some of the most populous parts of Papua New Guinea.* How did these inland peoples get there? It is tempting to speculate that many of their ancestors travelled via Lae and that the Huon Peninsula-Huon Gulf-Markham valley region was the focus of much early migration into New Guinea.

Where the migrants came from is uncertain, though archaeologists generally assume that they originated in southern Asia and travelled through Indonesia to New Guinea many millenia ago.[1] The present ethnological state of the Morobe District suggests that several waves of migrants may have swept through the region over a long period. The 107 languages and 27 linguistic families of the Morobe District represent two distinct linguistic types: along the coast and in the Markham valley various Austronesian-type languages, related to the large family of Malayo-Polynesian languages, are spoken; whereas inland among the mountains many of the languages belong to the older Non-Austronesian stock.[2] The existence of strongly contrasting physical types on the coastal plains and in the inland mountain valleys, and the differing life styles of these people, are possible evidence that the present population of the district came from diversified stock.[3]

When Europeans began settling in New Guinea in the late nine-

---

* There is some confusion over geographical names in New Guinea. 'New Guinea' is here used to indicate the island as a whole. 'Papua New Guinea' refers to the nation occupying the eastern half of the island, as distinct from Irian Jaya, the western half of the island, which is Indonesian territory.

teenth century the Lae were a small group of several hundred people, mainly Kawa language speakers, dwelling in about thirty hamlets scattered over a wide area between the Busu and the Bumbu Rivers. Lae was probably a frontier area for the Kawa, whose home is Bukaua* thirty-five miles east of Lae. The Kawa had been living on the north coast of the Gulf for many generations and had gradually been extending their territory both east and west for at least a century and a half before the first European settlement.[4] Apparently they occupied land that had not previously been inhabited, though it is possible that they rapidly absorbed any populations that may have been there earlier. The Kawa in outlying villages tended to maintain ties with the parent villages through trade, intermarriage and the celebrations associated with the *balum*† male cult; consequently most people at Lae had kinsfolk and allies in other Kawa villages.[5] The Lae hamlets were the most westerly Kawa outliers and their territory fronted that of the Labu villages across the Markham and abutted that of the Yalu and the Musom—related groups in the Markham and Busu valleys. Lae was thus an area where languages and cultures met.

How long the Kawa had been in Lae is not clear, though they probably came in different groups over a protracted period. Present village tradition indicates that some groupings are more recent arrivals than others. The fact that some families do not have full rights of land ownership but only usufructuary rights suggests that they are newcomers to the area. There are also dialectal differences between the families, and one of the early missionaries found that one group at Butibam regarded itself as superior to the rest because of the alleged purity of its speech. This is possible evidence that the origin of the population was diverse.

Local mythology also seems to indicate that people have been in the area a long time. Each group has myths to explain the features of its own territory. In Butibam the old men tell a story about Lo'wamung, the prominent hill on the foreshore near the present yacht club. Lo'wamung, they say, was once an island that lived in the south of the Huon Gulf. He moved to Lae because he resented the greed of his brother island, Bombiyeng, who used to grab all the best food brought along as gifts by local villagers. In every place where he had

* The 'bu' prefix in many local names is the Kawa word for water or river. Bukaua, or more correctly Bu-Kawa, thus means 'river of the Kawa'.

† *Balum*, a word common to many languages of the Huon Gulf, means ancestral spirit.

rested during his journey a large coral reef sprang up.[6] Lo'wamung has an important place in many Butibam myths. The two local creation heroes, M'de and Turu, giant brothers who performed mighty deeds, are said to have sprung from the soil there after an old woman had cut her fingers and thrust them into the ground to stop the bleeding. One myth tells how the brothers formed the saddle in the hill by cutting down a huge tree and dragging it to the beach to make a canoe; another relates how they killed a giant boar that was terrorizing the local people, preventing the settlement of the fertile land towards the Markham. The other villages have similar myths to explain their local environment: the Kamkumung people, for example, tell how Masa, a giant goanna which lived in a hole near the Bumbu, created the hills between the Markham and the Bumbu. When people trespassed on his land he killed village pigs and children, leaving only their heads to show his displeasure. The existence of a large body of myths and legends intimately linked to the local environment may point to a lengthy occupation by the present groups and is certainly evidence of their close familiarity with the land.

The scattered Lae hamlets did not combine to form a distinct political unit. Each one consisted of the members of a descent group who built their houses on common land, and each was a separate political entity under the leadership of its own head. Every hamlet consisted of perhaps five to ten houses. Individually the hamlets were weak, but they usually formed alliances with the other hamlets whenever they had to fight outsiders. Rivalries existed between some hamlets and occasionally led to fighting. The head-man, or *apumtau*, in each hamlet gained his position by merit, because as in most other parts of Melanesia there was no institution of hereditary leadership. He led by common consent and acted as co-ordinator of group will. He built up his merit among his supporters through his wealth, generosity and strength of character. He had a wide range of allies to support his claims to the leadership and won that support by working hard, planting big gardens, and acquiring large herds of pigs, which gave him the wealth to be lavish in his entertaining. Although he was not an autocrat he still had considerable authority, as he presided over the council of elders that managed the affairs of the hamlet and his opinion counted for most in their deliberations. The younger people accepted the authority of the *apumtau* and his fellow elders, whose dominance was reinforced by social pressures and the strong sanctions of traditional religion.[7]

Many of the activities of the Lae were co-operative as their work was hard and they relied heavily on each other for satisfying the basic needs of food and shelter. Mutual interdependence and reciprocal obligation thus formed the basis of most social relationships, and social prominence depended on the punctiliousness and generosity with which a person fulfilled obligations. Religious sanctions encouraged those who had received help or gifts to give freely in return. People who were slack in returning favours could expect social ostracism at least, and if they failed to mend their ways dangerous spells might be cast against them.

The reciprocity of Kawa society was evident in its social organization. There were two prominent social groupings: the matrilineage and the men's club. The matrilineage was important as the land-owning unit and from generation to generation the land passed to the men through the female line. Each area of land was the property of a unit consisting of the sons of the women who traced their descent from the original owner, the man who first cleared and occupied it. The average membership of a matrilineage was six men, who were all related to each other as brothers, maternal uncles or sisters' sons. In Lae each hamlet was probably a separate matrilineage. A man could expect to find helpers within his lineage to work with him on the agricultural tasks requiring co-operative effort—clearing bush for gardens, fencing, hunting, trapping, burning off—since these were jobs that concerned the landowners as a group. By assisting in such work he guaranteed that he would receive help from his kinsmen in return.

The men's club was concerned with much of the religious and political life of the community. Each club had a meeting house (*lum*) where the men spent their spare time relaxing or transacting business. Here a man could expect to find his best friends and thus assistants for co-operative activities such as house-building, fishing, sailing, and preparation for ceremonies. As a result club members were bound by strong reciprocal ties. The club was also an important agent for social control because the most senior members provided the village with its elders. These men held sway over younger villagers through the influence they had in their respective clubs. Finally, the clubs served as a mechanism for regulating marriages as it was common practice to 'seek a partner in another *lum*'. For these various reasons the members of different clubs formed distinct social groups within Kawa villages.

Like other Melanesian communities the Lae lived in a condition of primitive affluence,[8] making full use of an environment rich in resources. From it they obtained food, shelter and most articles of daily use such as receptacles, clothing, ornaments, tools and weapons. What they could not obtain locally—stone for knives and axes, clay for cooking pots—they acquired through trade with outside villages, using the fruits and vegetables their area was well suited to produce. Rare or special resources were jealously guarded by taboos. The site now occupied by the District Commissioner's residence, for instance, grew a vine prized as a canoe lashing, and the group that owned it kept others away by asserting that a legendary python haunted the spot and would eat any person, other than one of the owners, who dared to go there.

The material needs of the people were simple. The women wore a skirt of shredded sago leaves, the men a brief loin cloth of beaten bark. A wide range of personal decorations—ear-rings, wrist and arm bands of turtle shell, shell bracelets, pendants of shell and boars' tusks, and forehead bands of dogs' teeth and shell—supplemented this scant attire. Housing, like clothing, was well adapted to the hot climate. All houses stood on tall piles and had roofs of sago thatch, a design allowing for maximum circulation of air. Painting and wood carving reached a high degree of development, and it has been said that Huon Gulf art forms were among the most beautiful and expertly executed of the entire Pacific. Of all groups the Tami Islanders were the most proficient, and examples of their wood carving—betel-nut mortars, bowls, spoons, drinking vessels, spears, oars, canoe washboards and prows, balers, head rests, food hooks, bull-roarers, door posts, and house piles—are in museums the world over. The Kawa, too, were skilled wood carvers even though their work was less renowned.

Agricultural methods were typical of the primitive slash-and-burn cultivation of much of the lowland rain forest of New Guinea, a system that is primitive but still preserves a fine balance between the exploitation and conservation of the environment.[9] When clearing forest for gardens the people removed only the undergrowth, leaving larger trees. The main agricultural implement was the digging stick and this was used to break the ground only where vegetables were planted, in order to disturb the soil as little as possible. The ground was soon exhausted, and after one or two crops a new garden had to be carved from the bush. Hunting and fishing were important subsidiary activities. The men hunted pigs and smaller game in the large tracts of *kunai* grass. They fastened large nets to the ground, fired the grass and herded game into the nets with the help of dogs. The women used a variety of hand-nets to scoop up shrimps, small fish, and clams from the sea and the streams. During the fishing seasons the people built shelters near the good fishing grounds at Asiawe and Malawatup (at present the small ships' and overseas terminals respectively), where they lived while the season lasted. Hunting and fishing were the chief means of obtaining a regular supply of meat, because the only domestic animals—pigs, fowls and dogs—were reserved for ceremonial occasions.

The Lae, unlike their neighbours, the Labu, whose piratical raids on the vessels of other voyagers made them feared around the Gulf, were not great mariners. They did however build two types of canoe: a small dugout for local fishing and the larger *kasali* for over-seas trading. The foremost mariners of the Huon Gulf were the Siassi and Tami Islanders from near Finschhafen. Their boats sailed up the Rai coast towards Madang, plied the coast of New Britain, and penetrated far to the south in the Huon Gulf. Around the Gulf a complex and extensive trading system had developed, dependent on canoe voyages. The supply lines were far-flung, running across the Vitiaz Strait to New Britain, up the Rai coast towards Madang, and deep into the upper Markham and the high valleys of the Huon Peninsula. The distinctive feature of the trade was a specialization and concentration of certain types of production in particular villages made possible by the great variation in the natural resources. The Labu specialized in woven handbags and baskets; the villages near Salamaua produced sago; the middle and upper Markham and several villages south of Salamaua produced distinctive pottery forms; the Bukaua area manufactured bed mats and rain capes of dried pandanus leaves sewn together; Lutu at the end of the Salamaua peninsula provided a granite highly prized for adze blades; the Tami Islanders carved a variety of wooden bowls; while the Siassi Islanders acted as middlemen, trading Gulf products into New Britain and bringing back obsidian for knife blades and ochre for paints. The Lae joined in as producers of taro and fruits, and their canoes ventured as far as the Tami Islands and Finschhafen to the east, and south to Lababia and Siboma. Their best trading part-ners were the Labu and nearby Kawa villages. During trading excursions the small harbour at Asiawe, in front of the present Hotel Cecil, bustled with activity. The Lae maintained their canoe sheds there, and visiting canoes tied up there as well. In addition to the littoral exchanges most coastal villages also traded with those further inland. The inlanders and mountain people brought to the beach produce that the coast did not grow so well—yams, sweet potato and tobacco—as well as items of wealth such as bird of paradise plumes, dogs' teeth, and cockatoo feathers. In return they took shells and shell ornaments, pigs, fish and salt. The inland trade route at Lae ran through Yalu to the Markham valley and through Musom to the highlands of the Huon Peninsula.[10]

Kinship links around the Gulf greatly facilitated the littoral trade. Through intermarriage and migrations most people had relatives in other coastal villages, so that the men who embarked on trading voyages had many contacts. Even though women made many of the items of trade—pots, bags, baskets, mats—the men carried out the dealings. Trade remained at the level of gift exchange because commercialism was considered incompatible with blood ties. Kawa had strong similarities to the other Austronesian languages of the coast, sharing 66 per cent of cognates* with Yabem, the language of the Finschhafen area, 33 per cent with Labu, 32 per cent with Kela, the language spoken south of Salamaua, and 25 per cent with Tami.[11] Most coastal peoples could follow it and so it was the medium for communication.

The marriages the Lae contracted with their trading partners were an important means of cementing trading and military alliances. Marriage thus had an economic and political basis. The exchanges of traditional wealth—dogs' teeth, boars' tusks, household utensils, pigs and food—that took place between the bride's and the groom's relatives created and preserved alliances with outside villages and within each village as well. Some of the most impressive ceremonies and festivities surrounded the transfer of 'bride wealth' from the bridegroom's family to the bride's.

Within the villages marriage was regulated through the clubs, the men and women of which looked on each other as brothers and sisters. To spread relationships, marriage partners usually came from different clubs. Traditionally the senior relatives arranged the marriages of the young people, who had no customary right to choose their own partners. Apparently it was a satisfactory system for marriages were stable and divorce unknown. As with many other social relationships, reciprocity governed marriage. When a girl's hand was offered to a man within the village or to a man from outside, her husband's kinsfolk felt obliged to supply a wife for one

* Cognate: a word or derivation shared by two languages; thus 66 per cent of Kawa vocabulary is shared with Yabem.

of her male relatives.[12] The strong kinship ties between the Lae villages through intermarriage are seen today in land owned jointly by some villages and in other portions of land the ownership of which different villages dispute. They have also been accustomed to contracting marriages further afield, particularly with their close neighbours and trading partners, the Labu and Yalu, in order to strengthen ties with these groups.

The Kawa had strict ideas about marital fidelity. They strongly disapproved of extramarital sexual intercourse and had a puritanical attitude towards sex in general. Many of the traditional initiation rites for the youths and girls aimed at instilling the ideals of pre-marital chastity and post-marital fidelity. Those who transgressed were so soundly thrashed by their elders that few erred. Male adulterers were killed if caught, and homosexuality and prostitution seem to have been unknown. The sexual code had certain economic underpinnings. The people placed high value on virginity at marriage and a non-virgin was regarded as a liability by her relatives because they could not expect to obtain a high bride price for her. Polygamy was accepted as normal, though its practice was governed by economic considerations, as each additional wife constituted a large outlay; consequently only older, wealthier men could afford it.[13]

The various social and economic activities of the Kawa were closely interwoven with their religion. Kawa religion, like that of other Melanesian societies, was the cement sealing together different social, political and economic groupings, enabling them to hold together cohesively. Co-operation in the numerous tasks of village life was never a purely social matter, as every action had spiritual ramifications. Sex roles and dealings between relatives were sanctioned by religion; the headmen were not only the leaders of the social groupings but were the repositories of religious knowledge and the transmitters of religious tradition; economic enterprise was closely linked to social duties backed by religious sanctions; protracted periods of initiation and education in social and religious obligations marked the coming of adulthood. The myths and taboos relating to these spheres of action served to preserve standards of conduct and to maintain social control; and the man or group that transgressed too often would become the victim of sorcery.

The Kawa, in common with other Melanesians, believed in a host of spirits and supernatural beings—which for them were as real a part of the environment as the physical surroundings. Much of their religion was concerned with trying to manipulate supernatural forces. They explained the natural order by saying that there were a myriad of sky spirits carrying the heavenly bodies, the two most important being the creation heroes who carried the sun and moon and to whom most natural phenomena were attributed—languages, social organization, the distribution of resources, technical skills and the seasonal cycle. Among the more important supernatural beings were the land spirits and the ancestral spirits. The former, which could take physical shape, perhaps as huge snakes or goannas, would not interfere with the owners of the land they occupied but would smite trespassers with disease or madness. Therefore whenever someone had trespassed he made propitiation by offering valuables such as dogs' teeth, and whenever anyone fell ill his first thought was that he might have unwittingly entered someone else's land. The land spirits were also the source of much magic. Each descent group believed its spells, like its land, had originally been given to its ancestors by the spirits. In addition men called on the spirits of their land in time of peril, for that fortified them with the knowledge of what the spirits had done for their ancestors.

Like the land spirits, the ancestral spirits were also thought to occupy the land of each lineage. They were generally benign and helped their descendents in different ways, but might cause harm to those who neglected their obligations or breached village customs. Anyone who believed he had thus offended his ancestral spirits offered them some sacrifice to restore their goodwill. Burial practices were connected with the belief in ancestral spirits. After the burial the relatives observed a period of mourning during which they set aside food for the soul of the departed and lived in a house specially built above the grave. At the end of mourning they held a feast to mark the final departure of the soul for the dwelling places of the spirits of their ancestors. Strict taboos governed such sacred places, which were greatly hallowed, for they sheltered both the land spirits of the lineage and the souls of its dead. The deep attachment to their land which peoples like the Lae feel stems from these beliefs.[14]

Belief in magic was another basic tenet of religious faith, and the people accepted it as an everyday part of their existence. Different magical systems existed and the men of each generation received them as a valuable part of their inheritance. There were spells for weaving nets and using them for fishing and hunting, for canoe building and navigation, for gardening, for warfare, and to cure diseases and enhance personal beauty. All had their appropriate rituals: thus the leader of the warrriors always heated water and ginger together in a pot before a battle, and as it came to the boil he called out the names of the enemy. If the pot boiled on the Lae side the warriors attacked, because it was a sign they would 'boil over' the enemy; if it bubbled over on the enemy side first they retreated.

Sorcery, or black magic, filled a gap that might otherwise have existed because of the absence of institutions concerned with justice. Those who felt wronged had no recourse to courts and tribunals but only to revenge, which usually led to a chain of pay-backs lasting until the parties were ready to break the chain and restore the status quo. Sorcery thus served to regulate dealings between individuals and groups and acted as a safety valve for animosities. The legacy of this was fear and suspicion, and most deaths—even those caused by accident—were attributed to black magic. There were different types of sorcery, some more potent than others. The mildest form was intended to bring illness to the victim as punishment for some misdeed he was supposed to have committed; it was relatively harmless as it safeguarded the sanctity of private property and served as an escape valve for personal animosities. A more severe form was intended to cause the death of the victim. The sorcerer did not perform it within his own village—that would have reduced the number of helpers for communal tasks—but reserved it for enemies in other villages. The most severe form was used to wipe out whole communities.

The casting of spells called for counter-measures on the part of the victim. When he believed he was having sorcery practised against him, he performed remedial rites and set out to discover the identity of the sorcerer, who was usually someone known to be bearing him a grudge. Having found the sorcerer he offered compensation and if the sorcerer was satisfied he undid his spells. Where remedial measures failed and the victim died, his kinsmen sought revenge.[15] First they ascertained the identity of the sorcerer through divination. One method required suspending a bandicoot by its hind legs and then asking it who the sorcerer might be; the animal's convulsions indicated affirmative or negative answers. The divination probably did no more than confirm general opinion as to who had cast the spells. The victim's relatives then punished the sorcerer, perhaps by casting spells against him in return or even by killing him, which might lead to a battle between their respective villages. The people feared known sorcerers greatly, for they looked on their powers as dangerous albeit necessary. One of the great sorcerers at Lae was Mandab of the Tumata group, who possibly enhanced his reputation

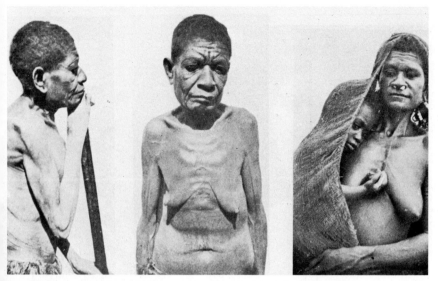

Women of the Lae villages, as photographed by Neuhauss, 1909

Wakang Endi and two Laewomba youths, about 1913

Magdalene and Gottfried Schmutterer, 1914

Schmutterer and a group of men from the coast on a patrol to inland mission stations, early 1920s

by living in seclusion in the bush, working his spells there until a group of Kamkumung men speared him about the time that white men began arriving in Lae.

The most important rites and lavish ceremonies revolved around the *balum* cult, which had developed from the belief that men and women differed spiritually and that only men could reach the state of sanctity enjoyed by the spirits. Women could not achieve this state, and so their contact with the men endangered the latter by drawing off their virility. The cult averted this threat and restored purity to the men. The central rite was purification through blood-letting by penis incision, which was said to drain off the contaminating influence of the women from the male point of contact. The men performed the rite before all important events—the construction of a ceremonial house, the planting of food for a cult banquet, a battle—and in the period leading up to it they lived in seclusion in the club houses, following numerous dietary taboos.[16]

Bloodletting had great spiritual significance as the Kawa believed that blood contained the essential life force, or soul, of all humans and animals. Many of their practices therefore entailed the use of blood in an effort to sustain and strengthen life. They smeared the bodies of the ill and dying with human and animal blood to restore the life force; before going on sea voyages or into battle they daubed themselves with blood or some red-coloured substitute and also ate dried blood or drank fresh blood to give themselves endurance; mothers whose babies cried continually coated their nipples with blood as they thought the crying indicated a deficiency of life force; and at various times they sacrificed animals and placed the blood in bowls over the graves to placate the ancestral spirits. The belief in the spiritual strength of blood also lay behind the ritual cannibalism commonly practised around the Huon Gulf. Any person killed or captured in battle was likely to be eaten, and every warrior carried a small sharpened stick with which he stabbed his victims so he could devour their blood and thus absorb their spiritual strength. If a party of warriors caught an enemy alive they usually brought him back to their village, where they would strike him on the head with an axe and drink his blood, thus ingesting his courage and vitality; they then despatched him with a wooden sword and ate him in order to assimilate his life force. The right hand was especially prized, and the victor cut it off with the least possible delay and devoured it raw.[17]

The central objects of *balum* cult ceremonies were bullroarers,

between eighteen inches and two feet in length, carved and painted
with secret symbols of mythological significance such as magical sea
serpents. The men used them to impersonate the voices of supernatural cult monsters, such as huge crocodiles. Women and children
had to run off whenever the bullroarers sounded, for these were
sacred objects and only the men initiated into the cult could view
them. Numerous taboos applied to the bullroarers. A headman
sending a messenger to another village gave him one to protect him
and show that he was on official business; and when parties were
sealing a truce or an alliance they exchanged them as a sign of good
will. Anyone harming a messenger or breaking an alliance was liable
to incur supernatural vengeance.

Initiation into the cult took place only about every ten years, after
a village had accumulated sufficient food to entertain a large body of
visitors and when it had a group of youths that had reached physical
maturity. The months of celebration and feasting, known as *sam*,
that led up to the performance of the initiation rites was a time of
strict taboo and anyone committing a major offence faced severe
punishment. This was necessary because visitors came from far away
and as their number probably included hostile groups the need to
maintain peace was uppermost. The *sam* cycle was a major trading
and social occasion as well, and people attended to exchange pigs,
meet friends and allies, and enjoy entertainment. As the initiation
approached the elders appointed some of their number to be
guardians during the period of testing prescribed for the initiates,
each of whom had a sponsor who had gone through the initiation at
the previous *sam*. During the initiation period both initiates and
sponsors underwent severe trials: at various times during the three-
month course of instruction and testing they received beatings, they
could eat only coarse, uncooked foods, they had to stay awake for
days on end, they suffered incarceration and partial suffocation in
rough and cramped huts built specially for them in the bush. During
this time they underwent long sessions of instruction during which
the elders warned them of dire consequences should they fail to
respect their seniors, or observe kinship and club obligations, or
refrain from offences such as extramarital sexual adventures. As the
time of final testing approached they heard the secrets of the cult and
saw the bullroarers for the first time, and bled through their first
penis incision. Finally, at the climax of the rites, lavish feasting and
dancing took place to honour the newly initiated men. The Kawa
women also had a number of rites which they practised at times

when their femininity was ritually at a maximum—at first menstruation and at childbirth—that is, when they were thought to be ritually unclean. At such times they observed dietary restrictions of different sorts and avoided all contact with males. The girls' entry to womanhood was analagous to the youths' initiation into manhood, though the rites were not as elaborate, and similar testing, ceremony and feasting took place. The period of initiation was severe on both boys and girls and occasionally initiates died from the maltreatment they suffered. The severity was intentional and served an important social purpose: it imbued the young with an awe and respect for their elders that they never forgot.[18]

The religion of the Kawa made heavy demands on them, as the many religious observations and obligations were difficult to maintain, and there were many onerous taboos. Certain kinsmen, for instance, were not permitted to address each other by name or to eat in each other's presence. Though such rules ensured that in-laws treated each other with respect they could prove troublesome despite being relatively trivial, because they were backed by religious sanctions, and an individual who unintentionally broke such a taboo not only had to make restitution to his kinsman but also propitiation to his ancestral spirits.[19] There were thus reasons why some villagers were prepared to abandon the traditional religion as soon as Christianity arrived: even though the new religion imposed its own restrictions and obligations, it offered release from the more onerous ties of the old. And so it was that the traditional Kawa system of interwoven religious and social duties held many of the seeds of its own destruction.

2

THE ARRIVAL OF THE WHITE MEN

During the last quarter of the nineteenth century Europeans explored and settled around the Huon Gulf. In this period a variety of individuals passed through the region: explorers, officials, prospectors, recruiters, scientists, missionaries and adventurers. It was through them that the peoples of the Gulf had their first contacts with Western culture. These early contacts, though spasmodic, were important for they established precedents which influenced dealings between the people and the settlers.

The explorers

Perhaps the first European to enter the Gulf was the French explorer, Bruni D'Entrecasteaux, who arrived in 1793 while searching for the missing explorer La Pérouse. He struck New Guinea near the island group bearing his name and followed the coastline into the Gulf, which he named after one of his officers who had just died, Huon de Kermadec. How much contact D'Entrecasteaux had with local peoples is unknown, as he himself died shortly afterwards off the coast of New Britain and left no description of those he met. After D'Entrecasteaux there is no further record till 1874 when Captain John Moresby arrived during his third voyage to New Guinea aboard H.M.S. *Basilisk*. He named the Markham River after the secretary of the Royal Geographical Society and began to examine the countryside around the river mouth but had to give up the attempt when he could not get his boats past a sand-bar at the mouth and found the banks too thickly wooded and swampy for an investigation by land. He was probably not the first European to make contact with the people around the Gulf for they 'seemed to have a knowledge of the white man and did not hesitate to come on board freely'.[1] At various places along the coast he found that they were anxious to barter with him and brought yams, tortoise shells and coconuts out to his boat in their canoes for this purpose. Black-birders,* bird of paradise shooters, trepang, pearlshell and sandal-wood traders, or any other of the European flotsam that drifted around the Pacific in the late nineteenth century could have preceded him. It is known, for example, that in the mid 1850s a party of Italian Roman Catholic missionaries spent a short time in the Siassi islands before being driven out by illness. In addition the German trading firms Godeffroy and Hernsheim were operating to the north in the Bismarck Archipelago in 1871 and had permanent stations in New Britain by 1873, and it is not unlikely that their ships visited the area.

Germans were responsible for the most thorough exploration of the Gulf. Their exploration began with the voyage of Dr F. H. O. (Otto) Finsch, who arrived in 1884 aboard the *Samoa*. The Neu Guinea Compagnie of Berlin, formed in May of that year, sent him to New Guinea 'to discover harbours, to establish friendly relations with the natives and to acquire as much territory as possible'.[2] He spent four months in New Guinea from September 1884, exploring from a base in the Duke of York islands. On one trip he entered the Gulf and selected the harbour now bearing his name as a site for a settlement. This later became the Compagnie's first base and the first capital of the German protectorate. The Finsch expedition was a significant factor in the complex diplomatic manoeuvres between Britain, her Australian colonies and the German government, which culminated in the annexation of northeast New Guinea and the adjacent islands by Germany and of the south-eastern portion by Britain. It sharpened Australian and British suspicion of German motives and helped persuade Britain to raise her flag at Port Moresby on 6 November 1884 and at other places around the coast, including the Huon Gulf, in the following weeks. Germany, equally apprehensive of British-Australian territorial ambitions, despatched a warship which cruised the Bismarck Archipelago and the north coast of the mainland raising the flag at a number of points, including Finsch-hafen on 27 November.[3] Finsch may not have foreseen the diplomatic crisis his journeys provoked: he was a naturalist who was chiefly interested in making scientific discoveries. His findings in the Huon Gulf were disappointing, however; although he later wrote two voluminous books about his 'ethnological experiences and dis-

* Black-birders were the labour recruiters who scoured the south-west Pacific in the latter half of the nineteenth century kidnapping men for plantation work in Queensland and Fiji.

coveries' in New Guinea he hardly mentioned the peoples of the Gulf.[4]

The most complete records of early German-Melanesian contact in the Gulf are those of the Compagnie explorers who followed Finsch. The Compagnie was granted an imperial charter to administer the new German possession and founded its capital at Finschhafen on 5 November 1885. The first Administrator, Georg von Schleinitz, arrived in June 1886, and during his two-year term of office encouraged coastal exploration, enthusiastically leading a number of expeditions himself, including a journey around the Gulf in the *Samoa* in October 1886. He entered the Markham mouth and sailed upstream for about a mile and a half. He was optimistic about its potential for development because 'the biggest ships could anchor right in front of the mouth. This spacious harbour, protected against all winds, provides a safe, secure anchorage'.[5] Like the explorers before him he seems to have had little contact with local people and did not mention them in his reports. His main concern was to find anchorages and navigable rivers and to give these German names. Many of the latter have survived: Dregerhafen, the Herzog Range, the Francisco River, Cape Gerhard, Bavaria Bay and indeed most points and bays along the coast have German names.

Two months after the voyage of von Schleinitz another Compagnie explorer, Captain M. Dreger, led a second expedition around the Gulf. He met many local groups and was the first explorer to mention those at Lae specifically. While anchored off the Markham mouth his party was surrounded by many people in canoes who 'behaved in a most provocative manner'.[6] They clambered aboard and had to be forcibly removed. Dreger and four companions later set off upstream in a steam launch and made contact with several groups of local inhabitants. While moored at one point on the north bank a large body of warriors swarmed around them and only retreated after several volleys from the rifles. Later the party went to examine the Labu villages, which were then built on piles in the Labu lakes. Pushing past a barrier of vines and branches that sealed the main channel, they entered a village and caught its residents hastily preparing to depart. Although the villagers were very frightened they greeted the party with gifts of coconuts. Dreger made several other important contacts around the Gulf. After a prospecting party he put ashore at Lababia was attacked, a retaliatory raid made under covering fire from the *Samoa* burnt twenty huts and destroyed the canoes. 'The salutary consequences of this step showed themselves in the strikingly friendly behaviour of the natives who were met in the next few days', Dreger wrote later.[7] News of such incidents probably spread quickly from village to village and this helps to explain the mistrust with which Dreger was subsequently treated. When the people approached they made what he thought were gestures of peace, offering dogs and holding aloft decorated peace spears, but whenever he indicated a wish to enter their villages they became hostile. He surmised from this and from their possession of iron tools and their eagerness to obtain further ironware that a party of black-birders had recently been through the district. No records survive to indicate whether this was the case as only a minority of Europeans arriving in the Gulf—the official visitors—left accounts of their exploits. Consequently local people could have had close dealings with a wide range of non-official white men.

The only other European to write about Lae in the nineteenth century was Ludwig Kärnbach, a horticulturalist and plantation manager, who went recruiting around the Gulf for the Compagnie in 1893. His account was the first to mention one of the Lae villages specifically. He anchored off the mouth of the Bumbu and was met by a large body of dancing, yelling people. They quietened down and peacefully came alongside in their canoes, however, when his interpreter called out to them. Kärnbach then went ashore and walked inland to their main village, which he called 'Lugamu' suggesting that it was in the vicinity of the present Butibam and in sight of Lo'wamung. He spent several hours there and learnt that they traded their garden produce with the Labu for fish. He also found that the Lae and Labu were allies and frequently fought with peoples further south near Salamaua. He appears to have made amicable contacts wherever he went, for he succeeded in engaging a number of recruits 'as a result of friendly trade with the natives'.[8] After Kärnbach there is a gap in the records on Lae, but it seems that by the end of the century Europeans knew the coastal region well and that the people had experienced their first taste of the West.

The Neu Guinea Compagnie

In April 1899 the German Reich relieved the Compagnie of its administrative responsibilities in New Guinea; henceforth it was to be simply a private commercial enterprise with plantation and trading interests. The Reich took this action because of mismanagement by the Compagnie, which had clearly been unable to carry out its commercial and governmental functions simultaneously. Although the Compagnie had taken almost no interest in the Markham area during its thirteen-year period of rule, except as a source of labourers, now released of its administrative burden it showed an active interest in exploiting the local resources.

The Reich gave the Compagnie favourable treatment at the time of transfer. As part of the agreement it undertook to pay the Compagnie four million marks, grant it 50 000 hectares of land with the right to select a further 50 000 hectares within three years, and to support its labour recruiting program. In pursuance of its right to take up land, the Compagnie now made a number of land seizures throughout the colony. One of its first and largest acquisitions was at Lae, where it seized 4743 hectares comprising all the land between the Markham and the Bumbu, from the coast to a line drawn between the two rivers about seven miles inland. The Compagnie asserted that this was unoccupied, ownerless, virgin forest. The claim was made by an unknown official on 5 April 1900, a year after the Compagnie had relinquished administrative control. The government had to check the claim and so Stuckhardt, the District Officer at Madang, arrived in January 1903 to examine the area personally. He reported that 'all the natives in the vicinity agreed that no settlements were located in the area and that no claims to ownership existed'.[9] The government now verified seizure of the land by issuing an Imperial Governor's certificate to the Compagnie in May 1903 and this had the effect of establishing the Compagnie's ownership. The Compagnie did little with its holding for several years and did not bother to survey or formally register the property, so that there was little effect on the people, who probably did not know that a large portion of their lands now had a new owner.

The Compagnie also had mineral prospecting interests in the Gulf, which it followed through the Huon Gulf Syndicate, a partnership it formed with the Diskonto-Gesellschaft to examine the rivers and mountains around the Gulf. The syndicate had a large and well-equipped field party of six Europeans and a hundred and sixty New Guinean labourers under the leadership of Hans Rodatz, who had been on several exploratory expeditions into the Ramu valley from Madang. They chose Lae ('Lugama') as their base camp and began work in October 1901, later moving the base to Salamaua because the open anchorage and steeply sloping sea-floor at Lae made it unsuitable. Lae was still retained for operations along the north coast. In the two years before the syndicate disbanded in 1903 it examined most of the river systems around the Gulf, including the Markham and the Busu. Although the prospecting results were not rewarding, the syndicate probably did much to teach the people about the West, as it was working around Lae for two years continuously and must have had frequent and close contact with them.

In 1907 the Compagnie again had an expedition at Lae. It was led by a surveyor, Otto Fröhlich, who had the task of determining the boundaries of the Compagnie's acquisition. Accompanying him was one of the best known of the colony's European personalities, Wilhelm Dammköhler, an adventurer who had spent thirty years farming, pearling, trading, prospecting and exploring in Australia, Papua, Dutch New Guinea and the German colony. He had visited the Gulf before, as a member of Rodatz's expedition, and in Papua had once saved his life on the Moorhead River by pretending to be a missionary. He had kept the local people, who tended to be hostile, amused for a fortnight by praying and reading his copy of Byron to them as if it were the Bible.[10]

Fröhlich's party spent three months at Lae and had close dealings with the people, employing them as labourers, guides and carriers. In addition it provided them with protection against their bitter enemies, the Laewomba people of the Munum area in the lower Markham. The arrival of the surveyors was opportune for the Lae, for it came in the middle of a period of protracted fighting with the Laewomba, who had killed many coastal people in the preceding months. Under the umbrella of Fröhlich's protection the Lae, who had temporarily abandoned their hamlets, were able to reoccupy their lands. Fröhlich and Dammköhler also gave them heart by leading them in a retaliatory raid against the Laewomba. The Laewomba had been prowling around the surveyors' camp at night and the two white men decided to take the initiative by shooting up their village. Taking with them a number of warriors from Lae and Labu they marched into Laewomba territory. Fröhlich left no details of the fight that took place, but apparently the raiding party won because he wrote that 'after this expedition peace returned to our camp again. The people dared venture into the bush again, which was not the case before.'[11] Previously the Lae would not go inland unless accompanied by one of the surveyors armed with a rifle.

After completing their survey in December 1907 Fröhlich and Dammköhler set out with fifteen carriers, including eight from Lae, to test Dammköhler's opinion that the Markham and the Ramu flowed in opposite directions along the same valley and that Madang was therefore readily accessible by an overland route from the Huon Gulf. The journey was easy and uneventful; it took only a fortnight and considerably enhanced Dammköhler's reputation as an explorer. The Lae do not appear to have understood the purpose of the surveyors' visit, though it is fresh in the minds of the older villagers today. Old men tell of the way in which the two white men used to frighten local children by striking matches. They also recall that wherever the two men went they hung red strips of cloth from poles, asking the names of all the local physical features and writing these in a book. They attributed this to the eccentricity of white men and did not associate it with a transfer in the ownership of the land. They were glad to have the surveyors for as long as they wished to stay, for they provided protection and brought valued trade items into the area.

Dammköhler is particularly well remembered at Lae, for he died in the area, the first white man to do so. A year and a half after the survey he returned overland from Madang with a new companion, Rudolf Oldörp. This journey, like the previous one, showed that the Ramu-Markham valley was well populated and fertile, eminently suited for agricultural development and the supply of labourers. In September 1909 Dammköhler and Oldörp set off again from Lae on a prospecting trip up the Watut, a large southern tributary of the Markham. They foolishly sent their guides back to Lae after several days, because of a shortage of food, and pressed on alone. They were attacked by a group of warriors from Babwaf village in the middle Watut and suffered dreadful wounds in beating off their assailants. Dammköhler, who was bleeding profusely from eleven deep arrow wounds, died the same night, 12 December 1908. Oldörp, hampered by nine bad arrow wounds, struggled to the river, where he built a rough raft. He drifted downstream for five days, once capsizing his raft on a submerged log; in all that time his only food was a cockatoo he had managed to kill and eat raw. Eventually, close to death, he was found by a Labu canoe near the mouth of the Markham. The local people cared for him until he was well enough to be moved to the mission station at Bukaua, where the missionary, Stephan Lehner, took care of him. When he recovered he left for Rabaul, taking with him a group of recruits from Lae. The attack on the two prospectors made a deep impression on the local people, for they had previously believed that Europeans were invincible.[12]

After the completion of the Fröhlich-Dammköhler survey the Compagnie gained full title to the property at Lae. The acquisition was entered in the land register (*Grundbuch*) on 25 October 1910, and after this the Compagnie did little to develop its holding. It was nevertheless jealous of its possession and acted promptly whenever the property was threatened. In 1911, for example, the first permanent missionary at Lae, Gottfried Schmutterer, wanted to set up his station on Compagnie soil and attempted to have a block released for that purpose, but the Compagnie, suspicious of the mission's hold over the local people, resisted all advances and when Schmutterer took up residence it moved smartly to dislodge him. In 1911 the Compagnie had trouble with the government too. The new District Officer at Madang, Berghausen, had been to Lae and had found a group of local people living on the Compagnie's claim. They had set up a village there after a series of Laewomba raids in 1906–7, because it was safer for them to live in one settlement rather than in a series of scattered hamlets. Berghausen now doubted the validity of the acquisition and directed the Compagnie to set aside a tract of at least thirty hectares to be given to the people. The Compagnie, through its representative in Madang, G. Heine, 'objected . . . most strenuously' as it believed 'the government cannot force us under any circumstances to surrender an area for a reservation'.[13] Heine nevertheless recommended to his directors in Berlin that they should grant about ten hectares to the villagers because he feared they would cause trouble if they were expelled; moreover the missionaries could be expected to create difficulties if the people were ejected. Heine's concern was ultimately in vain: within three years World War I had replaced German administration with that of Australia and in the general expropriation of German properties which followed the Compagnie lost its lands.

The Laewomba raids and Ahi migrations

As the first European settlements were being established near Lae, a period of bitter inter-tribal warfare that had begun in the 1870s reached its peak. The entry of the whites appears to have been a major factor in the increasing frequency and destructiveness of the fighting which took place in the Markham region. The instigators of the fighting were the Laewomba, or Wampar, a group whose ancestral home was on the Watut well up stream from the Markham. In the late

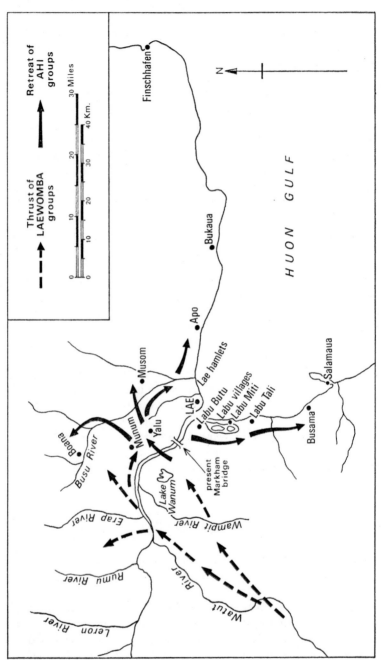

Population movements in the Lae area, late nineteenth and early twentieth centuries

decades of the nineteenth century they began pushing down stream, driving groups nearer the Markham before them. The Ahi, who perhaps numbered two thousand, were the main group affected. They scattered in several directions before their assailants. One group crossed the Markham and joined the Hengali people at Yalu, thus becoming the Ahi-Hengali. Another group, the Ahi-Wuru, moved downstream along the south bank of the Markham and settled in the area near the present Markham bridge, while a third group, the Ahi-Buangam, moved further down stream into the territory of the Labu, who gave them refuge. The Laewomba continued their advance into the Markham. First they drove out the Ahi-Wuru, then crossed the river and launched a series of ferocious attacks against the Ahi-Hengali and the Yalu. These groups dispersed, some fleeing into the Waing area of the Saruwaged foothills, some to Musom and others to Lae and the Kawa villages further east. At Lae the Ahi-Hengali received both shelter and usufructuary land rights, but although they were welcomed by the Kawa groups already there, their landless state was impressed upon them and has remained to the present day despite considerable intermarriage with the Kawa. The Laewomba now occupied the territory north of the Markham, setting up a number of villages there—Munum, Gabsonkek, Ngasowapum—then turned their attention towards the coastal villages. They began raiding the Labu, the Lae Kawa and the Ahi groups settled among them. The German ethnologist Neuhauss, who witnessed the end of the raiding, remarked that 'for a whole generation the Laewomba were the most feared murderers and arsonists among the surrounding tribes as they proceeded to take over a vast tract of territory'.[14]

The Laewomba raiding had dire effects. 'Larger and larger stretches of the Markham valley and of adjacent coastal and mountain districts became desolate and uninhabited and fear and terror reigned', one missionary wrote.[15] The Labu withdrew from the coast to hide in the far reaches of the swamps behind the Labu Lakes. There they eked out a miserable existence, often sleeping in the trees at night for fear of the Laewomba. As the raiding rose to a crescendo in late 1906 and 1907, the Lae abandoned their inland hamlets. Many fled east to the Bukaua home villages. About one hundred remained in Lae and resettled on the beach at the present Voco Point. Another group built further along the beach at Wagang, which they fortified with a wall of sharpened stakes behind which they retreated when danger threatened. Those remaining led a wretched life, a fact commented on by most early European visitors.

The raiders usually came across the low Atzera range dividing the Markham and the Bumbu, the most direct route between Lae and the middle Markham before the construction of the Markham road, then down the Bumbu. During 1906–7 they made repeated attacks, killing about one hundred and thirty people. Their most destructive raid, in July 1907, is remembered in local tradition as the Ho'mke massacre. They struck early one morning in a Kamkumung hamlet, some of whose residents escaped to warn the other hamlets. The Lae retaliated and a pitched battle took place at Ho'mke, a point on the west bank of the Bumbu behind the present Lae Technical College where a large outcrop of boulders runs down to the river. A number of the present Butibam and Kamkumung elders watched the battle from the shelter of scrub on the far bank. Mindering and Kising of the Wapiguhu family, who were about nine and five at the time, relate how their father, Tikandu, the Wapiguhu *apumtau*, was transfixed by a spear but struggled back shouting to them to flee before dropping dead. His wife and children in company with many other women and children fled to shelter with kinsfolk at Apo, about fifteen miles to the east.

Having dispersed the Lae, the Laewomba then proceeded to loot and raze to the ground the surrounding hamlets. Altogether sixty-eight Lae died in the raid. Fröhlich, who arrived in Lae two months afterwards, was appalled at the destruction. He walked through the abandoned hamlets and saw the cargo boxes, in which returning labourers stored the goods they had acquired while away on service, smashed and the contents scattered everywhere. Whatever could not be carried away had been destroyed, and 'in the riverbed of the Bumbu lay bleaching bones, broken spears and speared-through shields, the sign that a mighty battle had taken place here.'[16] Several more attacks followed in which bands of Laewomba armed with fire-hardened wooden swords indiscriminately killed whomever they could find. Eventually so many of the Lae fled or were killed that some visitors—Fröhlich and Dammköhler, for instance—at first formed the mistaken opinion that the entire region was uninhabited.

The Laewomba enjoyed fighting. It appears to have been both a sport and a means of gaining personal status for them. The warrior cult was strong among them and their champions wore round caps of bark cloth on which a human figure was painted each time a victim was slain. One of the first missionaries to visit their area found a tall post erected in the middle of the first village he entered; in it were embedded a hundred and fifty spears indicating the number of victims slain by warriors of the village. Their love of war thus predisposed them towards making attacks. They also combined pleasure with profit, using their forays as a means of obtaining foodstuffs, equipment and wives. A missionary who had visited some of the coastal gardens they had been plundering wrote that 'the scene of the deserted Lae and Labu villages is a sad one. They sow their fields and the Laewomba come and steal the harvest. The decaying gardens and neglected coconuts indicate the wildness of the Laewomba'.[17] What they prized above all, however, were the European manufactured goods—beads, mirrors, calico, knives, axes—brought back by returning labourers or given to village leaders as an inducement to supply recruits. In particular they sought ironware. Both Fröhlich and Neuhauss believed that because the desire to obtain iron goods was the chief motivation behind the raiding, the best means for obtaining peace was to establish trade links between the inland and the coast by bringing the Laewomba men to the coast as labourers; this would give them ready access to the trade items they wanted and would help in civilizing them as well. The fact that peace quickly followed the establishment of regular communications via the Lutheran mission stations at Lae and at Gabmatzung among the Laewomba suggests that Fröhlich and Neuhauss were at least partly right.

Labour recruiting along the coast was another likely cause of Laewomba raiding. From the foundation of Compagnie's settlement at Finschhafen in 1885-6, recruiters had been operating in most coastal villages. The recruiting was heavy and removed many of the younger, stronger men, the warriors, from the coastal villages for service on copra plantations elsewhere. As recruiting proceeded a serious imbalance of power developed between the inland and the coastal groups, making it easier for the inland warriors to emerge as victors in any engagement with men from the coast. While recruiting may not have been the original cause of the warfare—this was more likely to have been petty disputes followed by sorcery—it created a situation where a fierce warlike people such as the Laewomba were able to make easy and profitable attacks against the weakened coastal villages. Formerly a delicate balance had existed in which evenly matched groups had maintained relative peace, albeit precariously. This was now upset by European demands for labour and the introduction of European material goods.

The warfare produced marked changes among the Lae. One of the most important arose from the fact that fear of the Laewomba and the constant threat of annihilation so demoralized them that they learnt to lean heavily on Europeans for protection. As the raiding intensified they turned to any available white man for succour. Lehner wrote that often 'boys from the Lae district brought me news with tear-filled eyes: *"Lena, Laewomba seva aima lau getiam—* Lehner, the Laewomba have attacked our people again" ';[18] and Fröhlich stated that after he arrived they moved their huts to be near him. Having abandoned their hamlets they did not reoccupy them but instead remained near the beach and close to the whites. Later, after Europeans had imposed peace and many of the fugitives had returned, they set up the present five villages. Laewomba raiding and the promises of white protection thus triggered a transition from residence in hamlets of one lineage each to larger groupings where the lineages combined to form villages.

The arrival of a large body of migrants speaking a different language and possibly with a different culture was another change to which the Lae Kawa had to adapt. They demonstrated their flexibility by comfortably absorbing the Ahi refugees, who gradually lost their own separate language and customs. (After the foundation of the town the Lae continued to absorb numerous small and diverse groups of migrants successfully.) The arrival of the Ahi may have bolstered the Lae by providing them with new warriors, but another change that came about because of the warfare contributed to their state of demoralization. Living dispersed and under the threat of imminent attack, they were forced to abandon many aspects of the traditional culture. Wood carving and artwork, canoe craft, voyaging and deep sea fishing, dancing, ceremony, ritual and banqueting all seem to have declined rapidly. These were time-consuming activities that could not be carried on satisfactorily during a prolonged period of stress such as the years of the Laewomba raiding. They had deteriorated so far by the time of the first permanent white settlement in Lae (1911) that no visitors saw fit to comment on them. Their loss probably deprived the people of a strong sense of identity and purpose, inducing a state of apathy and depression among the people which many early European visitors found remarkable in comparison to groups elsewhere.

European settlement later restored the balance of power and provided the weakened people with protection, which enabled them to re-establish themselves. The introduction of Christianity gave

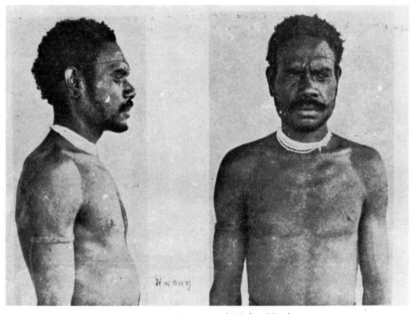

Uwaung, *Luluai* of Butibam, as photographed by Neuhauss, 1909

Lae airstrip and wharf with connecting railway, about 1931

The Guinea Airways hangar, with a tri-motored Junkers G-31 aircraft, about 1932. In the background is Lo'wamung (Mt Lunaman) with the tall fig tree that was a well known landmark before World War II

The Guinea Airways complex at Lae, 1940. The swimming pool and its windmill are in the right foreground. The large buildings left of centre are the Guinea Airways and Bulolo Gold Development hangars and stores. In the foreground are the mess, tennis courts and pilots' quarters. The black-roofed huts to the right of the hangar are labourers' quarters and behind them to the right are the married men's residences.

them new spirit and made them less dependent on Europeans. Until that happened they remained a disspirited people who leaned heavily on the favours of any Europeans they could persuade to help them.

The arrival of the missionaries

Missionaries first came to the Markham during 1906–7 as Laewomba raiding rose to its peak. They were members of the Neuendettelsau Mission Society, which had been founded in the Bavarian village of that name during the 1860s. The founder and pioneer of its New Guinea branch was Johann Flierl, an able and active man who had graduated from the Neuendettelsau seminary at the age of twenty and had then gone to South Australia as a pastor to the German community and missionary to the Aborigines. When Germany claimed New Guinea he obtained permission from the society to set up a branch in the new colony. He reached Finschhafen in July 1886 and received considerable encouragement from von Schleinitz, who helped him obtain land for his first station, at Simbang among the Yabem people, three miles south of the capital. Other missionaries arrived, and using Yabem as their *lingua franca* steadily expanded their influence along the north coast of the Huon Peninsula, around the Gulf and into the mountainous hinterland of Finschhafen. In its first twenty-one years the mission set up twenty-six stations, each staffed by a German missionary. The year in which the Lae station was founded, 1911, was the period of most rapid growth: in that year six stations were set up, possibly prompted by a fear that the Roman Catholic Holy Spirit missionaries might move into the Morobe District, which had exclusively been a Lutheran sphere of influence.

The mission grew according to a careful plan determined by Flierl, who held the reigns of control tightly during his forty-five years as the director of the mission. Georg Pilhofer, the mission historian, later called it 'the principle of wide meshed take over'; thus stations were planted two days' journey apart, enabling the mission to expand over a wide area in a short time. The areas between the main stations were then evangelized by New Guinean converts, allowing the New Guineans to feel that they were participating in the work of the mission.[19] Near Lae the Cape Arkona station at Bukaua was established by Stephan Lehner in 1906, followed by the opening of the Malalo station near Salamaua by Karl Mailänder in 1907, leaving a broad stretch in between for conversion by New Guinean evangelists. The missionaries soon realized the inadequacy of their plan at Lae: the population of the Markham was so large—Dammköhler's journeys had revealed it to be about 10 000—that a further station was necessary. Then the eruption of Laewomba coastal raiding in 1906-7 meant that stations both among the Laewomba and at the Markham mouth were needed to pacify the raiders and to save the coastal peoples.

Missionaries such as Lehner and Mailänder, who had to pass through Lae, heard of Laewomba depredations and saw the result in the abandoned hamlets, overgrown gardens and wretchedness of the remaining villagers. The appeals of the people for help gave the matter urgency. Missionaries visiting Lae were also impressed by the great interest the people showed in Christianity. Mailänder, who spent five days among them not long before the Ho'mke massacre, reported that the people followed him everywhere in order to hear 'about the great *Anutu** and His Son Jesus the Saviour. They also left their gardening to hear the word'.[20] They showed their gratitude, he believed, by giving him a canoe load of coconuts, yams and taro. He then made the best of their generosity by asking them to give him thirty rare ironwood tree trunks for house posts at Malalo. Lehner had similar experiences with the Lae. They appeared so anxious for the Gospel that 'almost every week they arrive in small or large groups after eighteen hours' journey in order to hear it'.[21] In addition about ten youths from Lae began attending his school at Cape Arkona. The missionaries probably mistook the people's need for self-preservation and protection and their desire to obtain the secret of European wealth and power for religious thirst; yet it was obvious that the Lae desperately wanted what the mission was offering, for whatever reason. The missionaries were thus compelled to respond, for a refusal to help would have exposed their message of peace, brotherhood and salvation as cant and hypocrisy. They recognized that to save the Lae and the Labu from possible annihilation, to accommodate the religious zeal of the people, and to preserve their own credibility, they had to solve the Laewomba problem promptly.

Their first reaction was to call on the government for police action against the Laewomba. This required an interesting rationalization on their part. Religious scruples prevented them from advising the Lae to strike back and from assisting them to do so, though they believed that this was necessary. At the same time they knew that a

* *Anutu* is the Yabem word for God.

foray into Laewomba territory would result in bloodshed. They therefore absolved themselves of responsibility by asking the District Officer at Madang to mount a punitive expedition, but requested that as many lives as possible be spared. The first such punitive patrol (*Strafexpedition*) took place in August 1907 in retaliation for the Ho'mke massacre. The District Officer and a Warrant Officer of police arrived in Lae with fifty native police and marched up the Bumbu and into the Atzera Range, where they pitched camp. During the night the Laewomba attacked the camp, injuring both Europeans. Next morning the patrol descended into the Markham Valley near Munum, but contacted no villagers. They nevertheless gave an impressive display of musketry to the empty village and although they later reported that they had produced a salutary effect by frightening the Laewomba, little was achieved because the raiding continued. The missionaries' attitude towards police action now changed and some of them later expressed the belief that the expedition was 'a deplorable failure' and that the police were 'completely wrong in attacking'.[22]

The missionaries were reluctant to pacify the Laewomba themselves. They would not carry firearms and believed they would meet hostility if they went into the Markham, as both previous excursions there—Fröhlich's and the District Officer's—had the purpose of wreaking havoc among the Laewomba. They knew it was pointless to send a party of Lae and Labu evangelists to negotiate peace. As a result they hesitated for a year and a half until their hand was forced by Richard Neuhauss in 1909. Neuhauss, doctor of medicine and amateur ethnologist, who was touring the colony compiling information for his vast treatise, *Deutsch Neu-Guinea*, was anxious to see the Laewomba. He was staying with Lehner at Bukaua and pressured the missionary into accompanying him. Lehner finally gave in and called on Mailänder and another missionary, Christian Keysser, to accompany them on a peace-seeking expedition.

They set out from Labu on 23 April 1909 in three canoes with about nineteen reluctant guides from local villages. The current was strong and the oarsmen were terrified and handled the canoes so clumsily that it took two days to travel the fifteen miles upstream into Laewomba territory. When they reached the first village they found no one about, though they felt they were being watched. They left gifts of boars' tusks, dogs' teeth, beads, sticks of tobacco and a length of cloth hanging from a prominent tree. They then lit a large fire atop a rise to attract attention, and departed downstream to await the outcome of their gesture of peace. The answer came on 9 May when a Lae man hurried into Cape Arkona with a Laewomba wooden sword. He excitedly reported that the Laewomba had received the gifts and wanted to call a peace meeting with the Lae, the Labu and the Ahi. The people now went ahead and arranged the peace meeting themselves, without the intercession of the missionaries. They met at a pre-arranged spot, lay down their weapons, exchanged gifts, and chewed betel nut together. To seal the peace two men from Labu and one from Lae went to live among the Laewomba for a time as hostages and three Laewomba went to the coast.

The Laewomba now sent gifts—bark cloth caps and a sword—to Lehner as an invitation for him to visit them. He and Neuhauss, guided by Wakang Endi, the leader of the Ahi at Lae, spent a week touring their villages in July 1909. Everywhere they went they were warmly greeted by crowds of Laewomba promising to respect the peace. At the end of the visit Lehner concluded that 'the unhappy state of affairs that has existed for generations in the storm centre of The Huon Gulf has reached an end, with the result that friendly communications can be opened up everywhere'.[23] It is most likely that the Laewomba were amenable to Lehner's overtures because they saw the mission as a source of European goods, and it is likely that the peace with the coastal people proved lasting because they now had easy access to these. The raids on the coastal villages ceased abruptly, though bickering between rival Laewomba factions continued spasmodically for several more years.

The mission now had what Lehner termed 'an open door' for the evangelization of the Markham valley and the country beyond. Equally important, the opening of the Markham permitted the entry of greater numbers of Europeans wanting to prospect, trade and recruit. The missionaries thus helped broaden the base for contact between local peoples and the settlers. The missionaries were particularly anxious for their intervention to produce lasting peace and they worried that the entry of other Europeans would hazard the extension of mission influence; and so when Dammköhler and Oldörp arrived from Madang to prospect through Laewomba territory, the missionaries feared their activities might undo the delicately-negotiated peace and set back the progress of the mission. The needs of the missionaries and freebooters such as the two prospectors were opposed. The latter were chiefly interested in finding gold; the establishment of friendly relations with local people was a secondary consideration for them. As they showed on the Watut, they could use their firearms to blast their way out of any awkward situation with little concern for the long-term effects on the people. The missionaries, on the other hand, had a more permanent interest in keeping the peace. Their success depended on their ability to maintain harmonious relations between rival groups, and between the people and other Europeans. They feared that an assault by one race against the other might lead to their own rejection along with that of other Europeans, and for this reason they were apprehensive about the arrival of prospectors.

To maintain the peace the mission now had to place a station among the Laewomba. Friedrich Oertel and Johannes Ruppert were assigned to this task. Early in 1910 they made a number of journeys inland to prepare for the foundation of their station at a place called Gabmatzung, near the present Nadzab airfield. While setting up their station they operated from a temporary base camp at Lae, the site of which had been chosen for them by the Lae. The name of this camp was Segwi, and it was on the low rise behind the present Titan nail factory. Segwi was on Neu Guinea Compagnie property but the Compagnie refused to release the area to the mission; Oertel and Ruppert nevertheless decided to risk the Compagnie's displeasure by occupying the site. The Lae accorded the missionaries an enthusiastic reception: Ruppert wrote 'They had been waiting for us and the handshaking seemed as if it would never end'.[24] The people thought that they, rather than the Laewomba, were to have the mission station and all associated benefits. In anticipation they had already built a temporary house for the missionaries and had cut the heavy ironwood piles and mangrove planks for a permanent structure. 'Such attentiveness I have never before experienced among the natives', Ruppert commented.[25] The impression that the mission was for the Lae must have been strengthened by the work the missionaries now undertook among them. They opened a school for the youths of Labu and Lae, began pre-baptism classes in scripture and Yabem, held regular services of worship, started building a chapel and laid out gardens.

In all of these activities Ruppert and Oertel received the ready compliance and assistance of the people. They were gratified by all the attention they received and assumed that it indicated a hunger for the Gospel on the part of the people. They were probably mistaken here, for the desire of the people for protection, for allies, for western goods, and for the secret of how to obtain these were important in rallying them to the mission. While the missionaries were fulfilling expectations by providing these benefits, the people were prepared to support them and were willing to heed their requests and obey their commands; but once they stopped meeting the aspirations of the people, they could not expect to retain the loyalty they were given at first. When the people discovered that the post at Lae was only temporary and that the permanent station was to be among their recent enemies, they quickly lost interest. The missionaries do not seem to have recognized the people's motives, and soon Oertel was complaining that 'the Labu are a right depraved company. It will really be a victory for the Gospel when they stop trying to find a way out of our instruction. One still expects to receive absolutely nothing from them without payment'.[26] Of the Lae he said, 'They would help us with greater zeal if they knew a missionary would remain among them'.[27] To get co-operation the missionaries now had to harangue and threaten: 'You have left your missionaries in the lurch, so why shouldn't they leave you sitting where you are?'[28] They could now find assistance in their many tasks only by deriding the people for their ingratitude or by making half promises that they would be given a permanent missionary if they co-operated.

The missionaries would neither heed the pleas of the Lae nor depart from their plans. They had practical reasons for moving into Laewomba territory first and were prepared to overlook the objections of the Lae until they had achieved their goal. The Laewomba district was more important from the point of view of mission strategy and had to be evangelized first; in the meantime the Lae and Labu had to be content with native evangelists. The people could not appreciate mission priorities, however, and were not satisfied by the rationalizations that missionaries offered them. They were convinced they merited a mission station and that their history established stronger claims than that of the Laewomba to the first station in the region. They pointed to their willing acceptance of the Gospel, their faithful observation of the peace, their youths at school in Cape Arkona, and their assistance and generosity to the missionaries over several years. They interpreted the mission's action as a breach of faith, and believing they had been betrayed they now sank back into their former state of dispirited lethargy. This became their usual reaction whenever they could not understand the purposes of the white man among them.

The Laewomba missionaries abandoned the Segwi camp and moved to Gabmatzung early in 1911, but Lae did not have to wait long for permanent status. Gottfried Schmutterer arrived to take up duties as the resident missionary in November of the same year. The reason for the mission's change of attitude towards the Lae probably lay in its need to service the vast Laewomba district without rupturing harmonious relations with the coastal people, through whose territory the supply lines ran. Schmutterer, who was twenty-seven, had been in New Guinea for two years, most of the time with Lehner at Cape Arkona learning Yabem and familiarizing himself with the Kawa. When he arrived at Bukaua, Laewomba raiding had not long finished and on visits to Lae he saw the result; he also met the people from Lae who used to visit Bukaua and was thoroughly familiar with the region and its problems. Except for infrequent leave breaks he was to be there for the next twenty-four years. The people enthusiastically claimed him as their own. They sent a canoe and two of their baptized Christians—Laegalu and Yalingnomsing— to fetch him from Arkona and gave him a boisterous welcome when he arrived, for they now had what they had been seeking for the past five years. European settlement, in the form of a Lutheran mission, was at last permanent at Lae.

3

EARLY EUROPEAN SETTLEMENT

After the foundation of a permanent European settlement at Lae the transformation of village society which had begun at first contact with Europeans began to accelerate rapidly. The main agents for change were the missionaries and the government officials who visited the area from time to time. Their presence satisfied certain needs of the village people, but it also created a number of tensions. The white men brought many new social, political and economic institutions and at the same time they suppressed many of the old customs. But the people had one quality which proved an asset: they were adaptable and were able to modify their behaviour appropriately as circumstances changed.

The German government

After the Reich took over from the Compagnie in 1899, imperial policy in New Guinea took new direction, mainy because of Kaiser Wilhelm II's pursuit of a more dynamic *Weltpolitik*. In New Guinea the new colonial policy meant an intensification of exploration, a vigorous native policy, and economic expansion.[1] This colonial upsurge, which coincided with the foundation of permanent European settlement at Lae, was suddenly halted by the Australian invasion, which unseated the Germans in 1914. It was only in the last few years of German rule that the new policy began taking effect at Lae.

The government had sent several of its officials down from Madang to examine the Compagnie's land claim at Lae, but apart from that had taken little interest in the Markham region until the outbreak of Laewomba coastal raiding, which it tried to discourage with the abortive punitive expedition of August 1907. It subsequently sent several more *Strafexpeditionen* into the Markham to punish the Laewomba for various infractions. The government's second such raid, in January 1911, was mounted against people who probably lived near Yangina, a village on the Langimar, a tributary of the Watut, to punish them for the murder of Richard, an English bird of paradise shooter. Berghausen, the Madang District Officer, incorrectly called them 'Laewomba'—for him that term seems to have meant any wild inland group in the Markham region. To punish them he marched in a party consisting of himself, a German Warrant Officer, forty-six New Guinean troops, and four hundred armed Buang warriors, the traditional enemies of the Langimar groups. The patrol punished with Teutonic efficiency: it burnt the village of its victims to the ground, killed forty of the people and dispersed the rest. A third patrol was sent out in 1912 to arrest Dammköhler's murderers, but could not find them, which was hardly surprising since more than two years had elapsed since his death. Such patrols had one main motive, the establishment of the Pax Germana (*Landfriede* or public peace), and the government seems to have been quite prepared to use any resources at its disposal to achieve this, to the extent of pitting traditional enemies such as the Buangs and the Laewomba against each other. Perpetuating traditional hostilities in this way and giving rival groups the opportunity of settling old scores was perhaps a questionable means of establishing the peace; it was fortunate that the mission was present and was prepared to intercede and conciliate between rival groups. Berghausen acknowledged the role of the mission here when he observed that a few missionaries had done more to preserve law and order in the Markham than hundreds of government troops.[2]

The punitive patrols probably had a marked impact on the people. Their destructiveness was intended to impress on villagers the omnipotence of the white man and the power of his government. People like the Lae, who had witnessed the firepower of several expeditions and leant on them for protection, were not likely to challenge what the government ordained for them. But although the government inspired awe and dread, it did not win the same degree of loyalty and respect from the people as the missionaries. The punitive patrols demonstrated the harshness and vengefulness of the government, whereas the missionaries appeared compassionate, sympathetic and placatory. The expeditions therefore defined the contrasting roles of government and mission for the people, and drove them into the arms of the latter. The missionaries themselves recognized this, and one of them later said that 'without doubt the expeditions helped the mission'.[3]

As well as its punitive expeditions the government undertook several routine patrols into the Markham for exploration, tax collection, census taking, recruiting, and the inspection of village amenities. Patrolling was an important part of German native policy, which was heavily paternalistic and aimed to protect, preserve and civilize New Guineans. The native policy was linked to the economic policy, which decreed that the New Guinean should serve as a labourer, pay tax, keep plantations and help with road building.[4] Patrolling was the chief means of ensuring that these policies were put into effect. Patrolling remote corners of the colony such as the Markham presented logistical problems to the District Officer, who was stationed 250 miles away in Madang, and as a result the people at Lae did not often see him. In fact the only systematic routine patrols he appears to have made were in 1912 and six months later in 1913. The 1913 patrol was the more thorough of the two: Berghausen made a sweep of eighty coastal villages between Kelanoa, on the north coast of the Huon Peninsula, and Labu. He used the patrol to draw up village lists, take a census to determine the age and sex composition of each settlement, collect tax, inspect village plantations, recruit police, organize road building, check sanitation, inspect the mission schools, interview the government-appointed village officials, the *luluais* and *tultuls*, and intervene in village disputes.[5]

By the time of Berghausen's 1913 patrol the entire Huon Gulf coast, from Finschhafen to Salamaua was under administrative control. This coastal strip formed a distinct sub-district of Madang known as the Finschhafen Organization. Lae, or Burgberg as it was known officially, was created a third-class station or temporary police post in that year. As a third-class station it had several huts of bush materials which were occupied only when official patrols were in the vicinity. An Organization was a region the government deemed to be under full control, which meant there was a *luluai* and a *tultul* in each village. These positions were supposed to go to the two most important men of the village, whose duties were to promote road building and other developmental works, to assist in enforcing the law, and to arbitrate in local disputes. The system of *luluais* and *tultuls* was probably not very successful anywhere, for as one *Annual Report* noted, 'unfortunately the chiefs appointed by the government are not always equal to the task . . . in the way that is expected of them. Among other things, they allow injustice and oppression to take place'.[6] The government nevertheless persisted with it, even though control through the local officials in some areas was tenuous, and by the time Australia took the colony from the Germans, the institution was an established part of village life.

How effective the village officials were in Lae is uncertain. The *luluai*, Wakang Endi, was a man of considerable ability. As a youth he had come to Lae as a refugee of a Laewomba raid on Yalu, and grew up to become the leader of the Ahi at Lae. During the period of Laewomba raiding he emerged as the greatest warrior at Lae, having killed thirty-six enemies in battle. He then served as the intermediary between the people and early European visitors—Fröhlich, Dammköhler and Oldörp, and the various missionaries—and accompanied Lehner and Neuhauss as interpreter on their peace-seeking journey among the Laewomba villages. When the missionaries settled in Lae they found him to be the most dependable of the local people. Their praises for him were high because they thought he understood Christianity better than the other villagers and that he revealed this in his efforts to maintain the peace. He was certainly a man whom few Europeans could overlook. He was tall, dignified and had a strong personality, so it was perhaps natural that he should become the first *luluai*. Nevertheless his choice may have revealed subtle undercurrents within Lae society that neither government nor mission recognized. There is evidence from other parts of New Guinea that the village official was not always the key man in village politics, but rather a man village politicians thought they could manipulate to serve as a buffer between them and the government.[7] Whether or not similar motives were present at Lae is not clear, though it is possible that Wakang, instead of being the 'Big Man' Europeans supposed, was relatively powerless. At Lae he was a landless refugee living there by the grace of the Kawa landowners. Thus he may not have played the dominant role in village politics, but may have been guided into the position by the head men of Kawa society, the heads of the various lineages. His receptivity to Christianity, too, may have resulted from his lack of ownership at Lae: he had a greater incentive than any of the Kawa to befriend the missionaries and embrace the new religion, as this offered him status and access to wealth which traditional Kawa society did not. Perhaps he also accepted the position of *luluai* for similar motives.

The tenuous hold the government had through the Organization did not, however, prevent effective control in the Markham. The District Officer seemed prepared to allow control to be exercised by the missionaries, who came to wield great power through the congregational structure they built up in each village. The congregation in effect became the agent for control and the missionaries the de facto authorities. Such a situation was possible because of the close ties between the district officials, the missionaries and the central administration. The officials always received a warm welcome at the mission stations and the missionaries wrote with some affection about them, particularly 'our beloved governor, Dr. Hahl'.[8] The missionaries were loyal Germans, so that a close bond was possible between them and the officials which did not develop under later Australian regimes, when mission-government dealings were marked by mutual suspicion and hostility. Berghausen's statement that the missionaries were doing more to maintain the peace than all the government patrols was a tacit admission that the administration of law and order could be safely delegated to the missionaries.[9]

Apart from maintaining law and order in the Markham, the German government gradually developed other interests there, and in the last two or three years before World War I began pursuing more active native and economic policies. In practice there were five main aspects to these policies: taxation, road building, the establishment of village plantations, the protection of native lands and recruiting for labour service. The aim of these policies was avowedly to protect the New Guinean and to draw him into the commercial economy as a participator in his own right. There was obviously a conflict of interests here and the government was not always able to reconcile its wish to protect the people with its desire for rapid economic progress.[10]

This difficulty was obvious in the matter of taxation, which took the form of annual poll tax of between 5 and 10 marks collected by the *luluais*. Those unable to pay had to labour on public works such as road building instead, at such low rates—20 pfennig, or .2 of a mark a day—that to pay the tax through labour required as much as fifty days' work. The tax, and forced labour in lieu thereof, were meant to persuade the people to pay the tax through cash rather than labour, inducing them to work for wages and thus for Europeans. The government viewed the system as a means of educating the people in the use of money and of encouraging them to earn wages as the basis for economic development. Whether or not the head tax did so educate the people is doubtful, as it seems simply to have been a means for their exploitation: it forced them to work for Europeans, then proceeded to take away from them the fruits of their labour. At Lae the government actually collected little tax because economic development was late in beginning and 'the people's production failed to return them the amount of their tax'.[11] Instead the District Officers imposed strenuous labour demands on them. Berghausen, for example, in 1913 ordained that 'in place of the tax the natives are instructed to build a 6-metre road the whole length of the coast from Finschhafen to the Markham'.[12] This was such a vast undertaking for the various villages along the route that it has not been finished to the present day; to complete it would have meant an investment of time and effort far in excess of the villagers' tax obligations.

A further means of drawing the New Guinean into the commercial economy was the encouragement of commercial agriculture on village lands. This took the form of the '*Kiap's** plantation', where the people were compelled to plant and maintain coconuts as a source of revenue. It was intended that they should use this income to pay their head tax. The plantations were also thought to be of value in civilizing people who suddenly had time to spare because of the cessation of fighting and the introduction of steel tools: their energies needed to be directed to other, more useful activities. European planters generally opposed the introduction of village plantations, because they feared it would cause a reduction in labour supplies, but in areas such as the Huon Gulf where there were few European plantations the scheme proved successful and the number of village palms increased steadily.[13] Around the Gulf the number of palms in the village plantations increased from 18 750 in March to 32 000 by October 1913. The District Officer reported that 'most of the plantations are growing very well and may be compared with any European plantation'.[14] He forecast an annual production of 300 tons of copra worth 120 000 marks by the eighth year so that 'the purchasing power of the natives will rise considerably'.[15] Unfortunately for the villagers these hopes did not materialize, because the programme seems to have been abandoned during World War I. This was regrettable for had the scheme developed and brought the expected returns it may have given the people some financial independence, removing their need to engage for long periods of labour service away from home.

The tax and forced labour, road building, and work for Europeans may have involved the New Guinean in the European economy, but one aspect of German policy that tended to exclude him was the land policy. The land law allowed for village land to be acquired by

---

* *Kiap* is the Pidgin word for patrol officer; it probably derives from the German word *Kapitan*.

Europeans but had safeguards to prevent the acquisition of lands necessary for the survival of any group and to disallow the appropriation of land without purchase.[16] In the case of the land at Lae these checks do not appear to have functioned adequately to protect the rights of the people, either because the Compagnie was determined to take up land regardless of the form of occupation there or because the government was not sufficiently assiduous in inspecting the Compagnie's claim. Lae was thus a case where the policy and law proved ineffectual, with the result that the people suffered material loss, though they did not see it at the time. When they eventually came to realize what had happened, their attitudes towards Europeans were permanently coloured. They learnt to distrust the white man as an intriguer, doubly dangerous because of the power he could summon in support of his chicanery.

The German policy that had the greatest immediate impact on the village society was that concerning native labour. The Germans believed that the most effective means of civilizing primitive peoples was to have them work for Europeans: presumably those who engaged as labourers would eventually return home bearing tidings of Western culture, to act as a civilizing leaven amongst their savage brethren.[17] During their patrols the District Officers therefore encouraged village men to engage. Berghausen indicated the official attitude when he captured nine Laewomba men as 'hostages for the peace' during his 1912 patrol. He brought them to the coast as labourers and predicted that 'in a year's time, after learning the ways of the white man, after learning the language, they will return to their villages', where he hoped they would have a salutary effect on their savage clansmen.[18] Perhaps such hopes were but a rationalization for the German need to use the cheap labour of New Guineans; certainly the rights of Europeans to New Guinean labour and their duty to civilize and safeguard the welfare of their employees coincided happily for the Germans. Few of them seem to have been aware that there was a conflict in the aims of economic development and the protection of the people. German labour laws strongly favoured the employer, who had the power to maintain discipline among his workers by imposing either fines, overtime, corporal punishment or imprisonment in chains. There were two types of labour: 'free' or non-contract, where labourers were recruited locally for short periods of service; and 'overseas' or contract, where the period of service was set for a longer time, usually three years, at places of employment removed from the home village. Control over the former proved difficult as there was no means for regulating it, but the government attempted to manage the latter by issuing licences to recognized recruiters and by insisting on obligatory contracts between the employer and labourer.[19]

Levels of recruitment around the Huon Gulf were high. Berghausen's census patrol in 1913 revealed that 82 per cent of the 138 men in the Lae villages and 78.5 per cent of the 141 Labu men had either served a term of labour or were away on service at the time. This was the highest level of recruitment in the 80 coastal villages he censused.[20] The government policy was clearly being put into practice at Lae: most men had the experience of working for Europeans and were thus contributing to the colonial economy, and whatever they had learnt about Western civilization was filtering back to their villages. The high recruitment levels at Lae were also important in tempering the relationships that developed between the villagers and Europeans. First, its frequency meant that it was one of the main agents for contact between the races and it was through labour service that most village men became familiar with the West. Their view of the white man was therefore that of the servant: the European man was an employer, a figure of authority who could mete out severe punishments and impose laborious tasks. It was a system designed to produce servility and unquestioning acceptance of inferior conditions. (This possibly explains why European men are still referred to as *masta* (master) in Melanesian Pidgin.) Labour service also provided the people with their sole source of cash income, a large portion of which then had to be paid out again in head tax. (The tax was set at between 5 and 10 marks; the usual cash wage was 5 marks a month, a third of which could be paid in kind.) Labour service was therefore significant in educating the people in the value of money. It also taught them the low value Europeans placed on their exertions, as the profit of a year's labour could be dissipated in several trivial purchases from a trade store of the Western goods on which they were becoming dependent—knives, matches, calico, tea, tinned meat. This served only to remind them of the omnipotence of the white man.

The Lutheran mission takes root

When Gottfried Schmutterer arrived in Lae at the end of 1911 he moved into the hut the people had built at Segwi for the Laewomba missionaries. He stayed there for about eight months, hoping that the Neu Guinea Compagnie would reverse its decision not to release a block of land to the mission. But the Compagnie remained unmoved and Schmutterer was forced to vacate his camp in July 1912. The people offered him another site, an area on the eastern bank of the Bumbu known as Ampo, which means 'wild fig'. It was owned by Wagang people who were prepared to release it as they thought it was inhabited by evil spirits; they did not use the land themselves because they were afraid of the spirits, who were thought to live in a gigantic strangler fig growing in the middle of the property. The mission purchased 100 hectares from the Wagang head man for 60 marks. Flierl came to Lae to make the purchase and Schmutterer and the *luluai*, Wakang, acted as the intermediaries between him and the owners. The establishment of the mission station on the new site was a co-operative venture shared between the missionary and the people. Together they set about clearing the forest, cutting the ironwood house piles, and carrying the sawn planks up from the beach where the mission launch had dumped them. By the end of 1912 Ampo boasted a missionary's residence consisting of a bedroom and a kitchen, a school, a dormitory for the pupils, a chapel, a cattle shed, and a coconut grove and gardens fenced against wild pigs.

The people followed the missionary across the Bumbu. Ever since 1906–7, when Laewomba raiding had driven them from their inland hamlets, they had been living in a temporary settlement on the beach, an area near the present Voco Point which they now refer to as Bualaha'ngkwa, 'the old place'. To be near the missionary they now moved to a place called Buko ('red water'), an area between Ampo and the Bumbu. They were to remain here for another five years until a serious epidemic of influenza caused them to move to the present Butibam site in 1917. The friendship between the missionary and the people was strong. He lived among them sharing their experiences, and until he married in 1914 he had no other companions. They recognized his personal interest in them and his efforts on their behalf in the school, in medical work and in visitation were appreciated. The Compagnie had begun putting pressure on them to move off its property, and as a result they had little hesitation in following Schmutterer.

Schmutterer quickly won the loyalty of the people and was soon making converts. The key to his success was his ability to embark on a variety of projects that captured their interest and demonstrated

The Reverend and Mrs Gottfried Schmutterer, Ampo, early 1930s

Schmutterer with some of his inland converts, about 1933

The Ampo Church at the time of its consecration in 1933

The Ampo Church, 1973. It is the only pre-war building in Lae and the timberwork still bears many bullet scars. During the war it served as a Japanese hospital.

the advantages to be gained from Christianity. His school taught literacy to the local boys, and he soon began running classes for adults as well. These were of two types: preliminary lessons in the background of the new religion, Bible stories and Yabem, and advanced lessons leading to baptism and confirmation, where the emphasis was on scripture and catechism. These endeavours were an immediate success, perhaps because the people thought attendance at lessons would reveal clues to the wealth of the white man. The school began with 50 boarding and day pupils, including several Labu and Yalu and a few from Tale and Tikeling to the east, and within a year the number rose to over 70. The preliminary classes for adults began with 60 but this soon rose to 120 and a year later there were about 230; the baptism classes began with 33 and had 80 after about a year.

The most impressive of mission undertakings were the baptismal ceremonies, which occurred about twice a year. The first took place in October 1912. It was a spectacular event and the people decorated their villages lavishly to greet the many guests, who came from Bukaua, Salamaua and beyond. On the Sunday morning the thirty-four initiates assembled, the men in white laplaps,* the women in white shifts, and proceeded into the chapel singing the Yabem hymn, *Jesus hold my hand.* Schmutterer preached, from Luke 12, the parable of the foolish rich man who wished to lay aside great wealth in this world in preparation for life in the next, and then baptized them, giving them the names they had chosen for themselves. Some chose Yabem translations of Christian concepts: *Jakamtung* ('I hold firm and true'), *Geputung* ('He protects me'), and *Gedisa* ('He is arisen'); others chose Biblical names. One man wanted to be called Kaisa Augusta 'because that was a great man' but was persuaded to take Johannes instead.[21]

A number of forces probably influenced the converts. Some may have been seeking a release from the exacting obligations of traditional society, others may have been seeking the source of European wealth and power; however, Christianity's message of peace and salvation also attracted a number. Wakang once confided to Schmutterer, 'My sin was pressing me to the ground, but you gave me the Gospel so I could become free'; and on another occasion, when his son had just died, shortly after being baptized, 'the joy in knowing

* The laplap is a length of calico wrapped around the body and reaching from the waist to the knee; since European contact it has been a standard article of male attire in New Guinea.

that the child had died baptized allowed him to forget the pain. He was firm in the conviction that the child was with the Saviour'.[22] The new religion gave such people a sense of hope and assurance. In addition the church offered security and refuge to those wearied by years of living in fear of sudden attack, giving them the stability they needed to re-establish their confidence. Protracted warfare, heavy recruiting and official imperiousness had left a legacy of list-lessness among the people. Their mental condition favoured the entry of a new religion and so they did not resist tenaciously. The missionaries often expressed their pleasure at meeting no opposition to the new ideas at Lae, whereas the Labu, who were more isolated, were 'not so timid and showed more persistence' in resisting the inroads of the Gospel.[23]

The mission owed much of its success to the manner in which it assimilated many aspects of traditional culture. The task of supplant-ing the traditional religion with Christianity generally proceeded smoothly because many aspects of the new religion had strong parallels with the old. Baptism, for example, was analogous to initiation into the *balum* cult. The long course of preliminary lessons and the oral test preceding baptism bore a strong resemblance to the exacting tests and instruction leading up to traditional initiations. The baptismal service, which marked the acceptance of the novice into the congregation, had similar symbolism to the rituals sur-rounding the transition of the initiate from childhood to maturity and membership of the adult cult. The baptismal festivities, attended by visitors from near and far, evoked memory of the *sam* cycle of feasts held during initiations. Confession and communion, the cen-tral rites of Christianity, were analogous to the ritual purifications of the native religion, as were the new marriage and burial ceremonies. The acceptance of Christianity did not therefore mean an entire and abrupt abandonment of customary belief and habit, and it was possible to accommodate many of the old beliefs within the frame-work of the new.[24]

The system of congregational government and discipline also re-sembled customary forms of group control. Matters affecting the congregation were decided democratically through discussion, al-though elders were prominent in leading this. It was the same method of decision-making practised in meetings of the lineages and men's clubs. Schmutterer succeeded in attracting converts by gaining the support of traditional head men, the most important members of the community, many of whom were among his first converts. Thus the leaders of his congregation were also the leaders of the traditional society. This gave prestige and status to the Christian community, which the missionary enhanced by setting rigorous requirements for aspiring church members. Converts had to attend the preliminary classes and reach a prescribed level of proficiency in an oral test based on the catechism. Those who did not perform satisfactorily had to keep repeating the course until they could meet the missionary's demands. He insisted on high standards for he considered that his congregation should be a prestigious elite corps, membership of which could not be taken lightly and was to be viewed as a much desired prize.[25]

The congregation maintained its prestige and quality by imposing strict discipline on its members. It supervised the religious life of the Christian community in each village by conducting devotions each evening and by ensuring fidelity to doctrine and adherence to the Christian moral code. Those who transgressed had to present themselves before a meeting of the congregation to explain their behaviour and the meeting could impose punishments on them. The sanction was exclusion, partial or total, from church activities. The more trivial offences—laxity in religious observances, quarrelling, dishonesty—could bring a temporary suspension of membership or denial of the sacraments. Total exclusion from services, sacraments and membership followed more serious offences such as adultery, bigamy, sorcery. An excluded member could apply to the congregation for readmission, and after serving the prescribed penance he appeared before the congregational meeting. If the church members were convinced of his penitence they readmitted him. The missionary's role in all this was ambiguous. He was obviously important within the congregation because he was the expert in matters of morality and doctrine. He had considerable influence with the elders and could insinuate his ideas into congregational discussions by lobbying them. Thus as the congregation expanded and claimed the majority of villagers he became a powerful figure in village affairs and was consulted on many issues. But though he exercised real power he remained as unobtrusive as possible; he did not wish to be seen to be meddling and it was a notable accomplishment for Schmutterer that he was able to maintain the impression that he was not directly interfering or imposing his own will. The successful development of congregational decision making was the basis for church growth in Lae, and in looking back on his early years there Schmutterer was proud to say that 'the most important thing is that the community exercises discipline and all things are discussed at the congregational meeting'.[26]

The operation of the congregational system could be seen in the case of D., an evangelist who transgressed by seducing a village girl. He was the head man of one of the lineages in Butibam, had been one of the earliest converts, and was a teacher in the village school. In 1914 the congregation excluded him both for being an adulterer and for being quarrelsome; but in spite of this he continued to give offence for two more years. As a result he incurred the wrath of the missionary and suffered considerable social rejection within the village. The pressure of this finally led him to regret his misdeeds and he came to the missionary and the congregation seeking readmission. A long term of penance was imposed on him, with the approval of the missionary, and finally in 1918 he was reinstated. At Schmutterer's instigation he was sent on a refresher course to the teacher-training school at Logaueng near Finschhafen, after which he was posted back to his school. By 1925 he had redeemed himself sufficiently to be elected leader of the congregation. In this capacity his undeniable talent revealed itself. He had a dominating personality, he was a persuasive orator, and as a head man had high status not only in Lae but also beyond. At district conferences of the mission he forcefully represented the Lae congregation, raising its status within the mission as a result. His congregation and his missionary counted themselves fortunate and praised God for his rehabilitation.[27] What they may not have understood however was that D., and men like him, by joining the church were probably serving themselves as well as Christianity, and taking advantage of mission facilities for reinforcing their own prestige and furthering their own ambitions. The congregational system, like traditional village society, favoured the emergence of such ambitious men who were concerned with getting to the top of society, from where they could exercise their power and influence. As a head man D. had probably been humiliated by his exclusion and rejection because his traditional status had been threatened. To preserve it he had no alternative but to regain his standing within the Christian community, for the church had become such an integral part of the village that traditional status and prestige as a Christian were tending to coincide. Social behaviour and adherence to Christian morality and doctrine therefore became inseparable and as a result villagers had to consider congregational opinion in all their actions. The missionaries believed they could see divine intervention in the redemption of 'sinners' such as D., though it is at least as likely that they were witnessing the operation of a traditional social mechanism that had been modified by their own presence.

As the church became grafted on to village society it flourished. With further baptisms the body of converts expanded rapidly and by the end of World War I the congregation numbered about 560 baptized Christians, or about a third of the people in the coastal region around the Markham mouth. The number of village schools increased from 1 to 7, and of pupils from 50 to 220 by 1921. Similarly the number of students from Lae in training at the Logaueng teachers' school and the Hopoi evangelists' school near Bukaua grew from 5 in 1914 to 26 in 1918. The emergence of a class of trained teachers and evangelists among the Lae meant that the congregation became self-sustaining. This gave the local church a high degree of autonomy and encouraged a sense of corporate identity among the people. They began feeling a group pride and self respect which had disappeared during the period of early European contact and Lae-womba raiding. The new mood among the Lae revealed itself in a number of ways. By 1921 Schmutterer was reporting that 'more self assurance and a sense of responsibility is building up among the con-gregation'.[28] In addition a new feeling of unity was growing for 'the earlier frictions between the Lae clans have disappeared'.[29]

An important factor in the revival of the Lae was the extension of the mission beyond the local villages into the mountainous hinter-land. This movement began at the end of 1915 when the Lae con-gregation sent out eight of its members to serve as evangelists in converting the Laewomba. In addition two more went to Musom, a vantage point in the foothills to the north for entry into the extensive and populous valley system of the Saruwaged Ranges. After Musom the next goals were stations in the Nabak and Waing regions beyond; these were opened in 1917 and 1918 respectively. The Lae congregation now had a mission field of its own and could send out its own evangelists. This had a significant effect on the Lae. It enabled them to regard themselves with new esteem, for they could now view themselves as the vanguard of the Christian assault on paganism, an elite whose noble duty it was to enlighten the ignorant and backward peoples of the mountains. This high calling gave them a new purpose and direction, which they pursued with zest. Their refreshed vitality was apparent in the challenge issued by an evangelist at church one Sunday: 'I am going to the inland to visit the heathen. Who is coming with me?'[30] So enthusiastically was the challenge taken up that by 1922 the congregation was providing the finance for the support of evangelists at ten inland outposts.

The fostering of such a fine esprit de corps had not proceeded with complete ease, for Christianity had met certain set-backs along the way. One of the earliest difficulties was linguistic. The congregation spoke five languages and dialects (Kawa, Labu, Aliwadza, Yalu and Musom), and so the first task for the missionaries was to impose Yabem, the church language. Instruction in Yabem was always a part of the preliminary baptismal classes, but only the Kawa, whose language is very close to Yabem, learnt it easily. The Labu resisted. Schmutterer wrote, 'They often say to me, "Speak our language" but this of course was not possible for the mission could not use a language for only a couple of hundred people'.[31] Christianity spread more slowly among them as a result. He persisted in imposing Yabem through the school and baptismal lessons, however, and 'gradually they gave in and learnt Jabêm and the Gospel together'.[32]

Another early problem was the opposition of elderly villagers who were steeped in the old religion and resented the intrusion of the new. Such a man was Dikawi, the Labu *tultul*, who steadfastly refused the offer of baptism as he lay dying. His last words were: 'I have never believed the Gospel and I am going to the ancestors in their place.'[33] Another old Labu man, a sorcerer, tried to discourage the local youths from attending the school, promising a swift death if they learnt to read and write. He was jealous of his hold over the young and did not want the mission to loosen it. Gradually the opposition of such men disappeared and many embraced the new religion, symbolically destroying their parcels of magic-making materials.[34] Perhaps they realized that the rapid spread of the new religion had made an anachronism of the sorcerer's craft, so that joining the church was the line of least resistance.

One obstacle that persisted, and still remains today, was the traditional rivalry between various groups in the congregation. The main division was that between the Labu and the Lae, but there were also divisions between and within the numerous Kawa and Ahi lineages at Lae. In Lae the lineages had only just abandoned their separate hamlets and come together as villages. It took many years before the people were able to lose their identity with particular lineages and to feel a wider loyalty to the village. One way in which old rivalries revealed themselves was in fighting over football. The lineages used to play against each other and matches often ended with brawling. One of the present head men of Butibam is still crippled from the injuries he suffered nearly sixty years ago in a fight following a match. The division between the Lae and the Labu was of greater magnitude. Their rivalry was serious despite their marriage and trade links, and before European contact they had vacillated between enmity and uneasy alliance. With the coming of Christianity the Lae became the foundation of the congregation. The Labu were isolated on the far side of the Markham and often contrary winds and tides, the deep Gulf swell, and Markham floods kept them away from services at Ampo for weeks on end, and so they made only slow progress into Christianity. As a result the Lae used to jeer at them for being primitive and heathen; this exacerbated old rivalries so that bickering was not uncommon between the two groups. The most notable dispute was in 1917 when fighting broke out between rival groups of youths from Lae and Labu who had returned from service with the police. The quarrel had begun while they were away on duty when the Lae had made slighting remarks about the Labu. The congregation split over the dispute and the Christians took sides, sundering the brotherhood Schmutterer imagined he could detect in 1916 when he wrote that 'the inner life of the congregation has made pleasing progress because the different tribes perceive that they must draw together if they are to advance'.[35] In this case at least the church had become an agent for perpetuating old animosities, and even though the missionaries from time to time stated their belief that a sense of community was developing between the Lae and Labu, similar disputes continued to divide them both within and without the church.

The old religion was another aspect of the traditional culture that did not die easily. The people took up Christianity enthusiastically, but vestiges of their former faith emerged periodically, especially at times of crises. Belief in the old spirits, in magic and sorcery was anathema to the missionaries and they were determined to root it out for it challenged the whole basis of their vocation. They were determined to impose Lutheran orthodoxy and would not tolerate deviation. At times their strength of purpose made them unsympathetic to the needs of the people when these were expressed through non-Christian means. Not long after Schmutterer arrived in Lae he noted with disdain that 'in the first few nights in Lae I had the pleasure of listening to the howling and lamentations over the death of a favourite hunting dog. The two Christians that came with me from Bukaua helped me to restore order'.[36] Then in 1917 when a serious epidemic of influenza killed about eighty people and the prayers of the congregation were unable to halt the mounting death toll, some villagers began looking for an explanation in the old faith. He brusquely dismissed their ideas with little sympathy for their confusion: 'the sinister rumours and ridiculous talk were started by the heathen'.[37] And as late as 1923 he was piqued to observe that 'the coastal people might condemn their old sins but they continue to follow their old ways and continue to plant their yams with human bones'.[38] These fulminations against the retention of the old beliefs indicated an inflexibility on the part of the missionary and a lack of understanding of the deepest needs of his flock. He could not appreciate that the traditional religion was implicit in nearly every facet of village life and that simply railing against it was therefore in vain. It would continue to reappear whenever the need arose until Christianity had so thoroughly permeated the village society that the people could rely on that instead.

The mounting pace of change

As the mission overcame its early obstacles and gained a firmer hold over the people it introduced new ideas and institutions, changed and modified some of the older customs, and strengthened others. As it did this it wrought a number of changes in the village society.

Marriage and sexual morality were areas where these tendencies could be observed. Traditional morality was puritanical, and so the Lutheran ethic was clearly understood and adopted without question. This explains why transgressors such as D. received summary treatment from the congregational meeting. But the mission also introduced new concepts such as monogamy. Before the arrival of the missionaries polygamy had been general, and the older, wealthier men at least had more than one wife. The missionaries would not tolerate polygamy and would baptize only the monogamous men or those who had divorced their extra wives. Ironically, they thus introduced the concept of divorce although they preached about the 'indissolubility of marriage': in demanding that converts put away their additional wives they taught the people what divorce was. They considered that true Christian faith would reveal itself in the convert's willingness to put aside his other wives. Wakang impressed them with this type of fidelity. Oertel wrote, 'That there are honest, responsible people among the Lae is shown to our joy in our faithful old interpreter, Wakang, who is ahead of them all and without urging released his second and third wives'.[39] ('Release' was the mission's euphemism for divorce.) The ruling on monogamy was hardest on divorced wives. They were left shamed and without support, and even though the mission tried to secure husbands for them they felt disgraced, particularly if they had children, who had become illegitimate as a result. Schmutterer found that the divorced wives flocked to his baptismal classes, weeping that he had caused their divorce and was therefore bound to look after them.[40] The missionaries prosecuted their policy vigorously: any man taking extra wives was promptly excluded and his wives with him. As a result polygamy disappeared within several years, but until it did it caused great anguish for the divorced wives.

Although the missionaries' morality was adopted readily, they unwittingly created the conditions for a breaching of their own code. The evangelists and the teachers, those bearers of the new morality, were also the most prone to lapse from it. D. was but the first to fall, and as the mission field opened up there were further cases. Many of the workers on the mission outposts were young unmarried men or men who had left their wives in Lae. A problem arose when such men were posted to remote areas to work among people they probably regarded as inferiors and whose sexual morality may not have been as puritanical as their own. Freed from the normal restraints of their own society, and probably given some allure by virtue of their high status, the mission workers were exposed to severe temptations. The list of those who succumbed was long and included one of the mission's most trusted and reliable converts. A typical case was that of N., an early convert who helped Schmutterer pioneer the Waing and a man he described as 'very gifted, fearless and enterprising'.[41] After several years at the outpost N.'s wife fell ill and returned to Lae. In her absence N. formed a number of liaisons with Waing women whose men were away on labour service. The congregation withdrew him and excluded him, but after several months he applied for readmission. They allowed him to return to services of worship but suspended him from communion for a further period and banned him from ever returning to the Waing. Such cases caused the missionaries great heart-burning and brought severe punishments from the congregation, for the lapse of an evangelist undermined the reputation of both mission and congregation. Nevertheless similar misdemeanours continued and no amount of discipline seemed able to prevent them.

Among the greatest changes the mission wrought on the village society were those that came through education. Although the mission school started in a small way, it drew its pupils from a wide area—Lae, Labu, Yalu, Musom, Tale, Tikeling—and its numbers rose steadily. By 1916 when Schmutterer wrote that 'the need for the school is now fully and completely appreciated and only in two backward villages have the old heathens caused trouble', other schools were being opened in the villages because the Ampo school could no longer handle the increase.[42] The schools taught literacy in Yabem, arithmetic and scripture. They were staffed by teachers who had been through the schools themselves and then undergone further training at Logaueng. Most of the teachers were from the local congregation and there was always a small group of students at the training school to allow for replacements and expansion. The men attracted in to the service of the mission were mostly intelligent, able young fellows. What led them to offer themselves is not clear. Perhaps they felt they had been called by God, but it is also likely that they were prompted by the benefits accruing to those who joined: mission workers were supported by the rest of the community and did not have to do physical work; in addition their position was respected and they gained high status at home and abroad. The teachers and evangelists were a new class within the village society, a group that did not tend gardens, fish, hunt or build like other villagers. The idea of a specialized elite—canoe builders, navigators, sorcerers—had existed within the traditional society, but the existence of a class which produced no material goods was novel. The teachers imposed a responsibility on the community, which now had to feed them or provide them with garden land. They suffered if this duty was observed tardily and one of the early difficulties was to persuade the villagers to honour their obligations to the teachers. However, the missionaries worked on the problem and eventually the people learnt to regard the support of the teachers as one of their Christian duties.

Literacy spread rapidly via the schools and by 1926 Schmutterer was able to boast that the enthusiasm for education was so keen that for years most children in the villages had been attending school and all the young people entering confirmation classes could 'write almost without mistake and could read the new Testament'.[43] This soon began having an important effect on the villages, which now contained a new class of young, literate people whose education was separating them from their elders. The young people, unlike their parents, were growing up in the shadow of the mission. They only had a second-hand knowledge of the traditional religion and the heavy sanctions it relied on, and therefore were not as ready to accept the will of the elders as earlier generations had been. Even though the new literacy was confined to the Testaments and catechism, it gave the young people skill and knowledge their parents did not share. The missionaries were driving a wedge between the genera-tions and before long there would be complaints that the younger generation was displaying less and less respect for the old and that many of the old valued customs were crumbling because of this.

Another significant change introduced by the mission was the con-cept of day or wage labour. Although contract labour and recruiting had been part of village experience for several decades, there was no avenue for local employment other than carrying for occasional European visitors until the mission founded Malahang plantation one and a half miles east of Ampo in 1914. This plantation, occupy-ing 1500 acres, was the largest of the mission's three plantations on the Huon Gulf and eventually contained 30 000 palms.[44] Malahang provided numerous opportunities for employment, which meant that village men could now work near home to earn money rather than engage for service in distant places and for long periods of absence from the village. Work for the mission proved popular and by 1917 Malahang had a labour force of fifty, and by 1920 this had risen to eighty-five. The plantation brought a change in the relation-ship between the mission and the village community. The mission was now both a commercial enterprise and an employer, which meant a more formal connection with the village men. In following its role as entrepreneur the mission had to recruit labourers in the same way as any planter or company, it had to observe the same labour regulations, and similarly it had to protect its own interests by disciplining lax employees. A number of minor incidents indicated the growing formality of the relationship. In one the missionary in charge of the plantation prosecuted a group of his employees, some of whom were members of the congregation, for stealing from the plantation vegetable garden; in another, one of the employees prose-cuted the missionary for forcing him to work when he was unwell. The effect of incidents such as these was to define sharply the respec-tive roles of the mission as employer and the congregational member as employee, thus creating tensions in what had previously been a close fraternal bond. Furthermore the government now became a party to one aspect of the mission-village relationship, as it had the right to intervene and ensure due observance of the labour regulations. This later became important as government and mission began vying for the loyalty of the people.

As the missionaries consolidated their influence around the Gulf they encouraged a sense of fraternity and common identity between the coastal people. Perhaps this had existed before European contact, fostered by trade and intermarriage, but the Yabem language and the unity of the missionaries—all of whom had graduated from the same Bavarian seminary—did a great deal to develop it. One of their most significant contributions in this direction was an annual conference of the congregations which they instituted under the name of Melanesian Day. It had 'the main purpose of bringing together congregations that were once divided by clan and tribal differences . . . to come close together and think of uniting in Christ.'[45] The first two conferences took place at Bukaua in 1911 and 1914. The third was at Lae in 1916 and thereafter they were held annually, at a different place to enable every congregation to act as host in turn. Each conference was built around a particular theme; thus the first one at Lae considered differences between the Melanesian (Yabem language) and Papuan or Non- Melanesian (Kâte language) mission districts* and the best means of co-operation between them. Discussions were not restricted to purely religious affairs but extended to all matters affecting the life of the congregations. The relationship between the civil authorities and the congregations was a common theme and many villagers used the occasion to give vent to their complaints about the government. The conferences had a strong didactic bias and were used to spread mission propaganda. At one of them, for example, two groups staged a highly dramatic mock battle, at the end of which they burnt their swords, spears and shields 'to show the young people that the old heathen stuff does not go with the new beliefs'.[46]

Melanesian Day became one of the main events in the mission calendar and still is. The people looked forward to it as a huge festival in which the various host congregations vied with each other to provide hospitality for the hundreds of guests. Apart from its religious function it gave the people an opportunity for social inter-

---

* In the Morobe District the Lutherans used Yabem as their coastal *lingua franca* among the peoples speaking Melanesian, that is Austronesian languages; but in the hills, where most peoples spoke Non-Austronesian (sometimes referred to as 'Papuan') languages, they used Kâte, a Non-Austronesian language of the Sattelberg area behind Finschhafen.

course and informal bargaining. At the first Lae festival, for example, the Labu representatives tried to persuade the Lae to provide them with food whenever they came across the Markham for church services, and at the 1918 conference the Bukaua proposed that outside villages should be much more liberal in allowing their girls to marry into Bukaua families. In addition Melanesian Day took on the function of the pig market, or *sam*, that used to be a part of the gatherings organized around the initiations into the *balum* cult. When the people began using the conferences for exchanging pigs, the missionaries saw the value of strengthening the Christian festival with practices of the pagan cult, though they insisted that the traditional rites be eliminated from the exchange. By so investing a traditional practice with new significance, the mission succeeded in affirming the strength of the congregations. A further advantage was that the conference strengthened the people's assurance in the new religion. The missionaries realized that if Christianity were to take root in Melanesian society permanently it had to become self-sustaining. For this reason they took a back seat at *Sam*, offering advice but encouraging the congregational representatives to manage the programme themselves. As a result participants gained confidence with each successive gathering.[47]

Thus in its first decade the mission had succeeded in binding itself inextricably to the village society. The people readily adopted the new faith because its concepts and institutional forms were analogous to those of traditional society and because it offered benefits which promised to stabilize local conditions and promote their interests. It also gave them new drive and direction and enabled them to regain their self confidence. However, at the same time it brought them new tensions. Those who rejected its authority were in turn rejected by the congregation. Those who opposed its expansion at the expense of the old religion became an isolated, alienated minority. Those who manned its remote outposts were the most apt to fall short of its demanding moral standards and thus had to face humiliation and rejection at home and on their stations. It opened up a division between the old and young which traditional society had not permitted. And finally, as the missionaries became more concerned with the problems of the growth of the out-stations and of the mission's commercial ventures, their earlier personal relationship diminished and became formalized.

In the first years of European settlement the Lae had been anxious for white men to settle amongst them for the advantages they thought this would bring. When both government and mission arrived they realized that Western civilization had two faces: the officials demanded obedience, respect and passiveness and this contrasted strongly with the accommodating manner of the missionaries. It was therefore the missionaries who received the early loyalty and avid support of the people. It was only in later years that they realized that government and mission were but two sides of the same coin, and that both wished to shape them into preconceived moulds, the ultimate end of which was transformation of their village society.

4

THE AUSTRALIANS ENTER LAE

The arrival of the Australian Naval and Military Expeditionary Force at Rabaul in September 1914 at the outbreak of World War I suddenly ended thirty years of German rule in New Guinea. Within a week of arriving the Australian invaders had stilled the opposition of the Germans and had taken over their administration without major dislocation.[1] Although the military takeover was hardly noticed at Lae, which was one of the more remote outposts of the colony, the change in administrations was soon to have important consequences for the local community.

The Australian military regime

When the Australians captured New Guinea they were ill prepared for their colonial task. Having but recently emerged from colonialism themselves, they had little experience in colonial administration. Their first years in New Guinea were therefore a time of trial end error. To the Germans who remained they seemed brash, inept and uninspired by any over-riding colonial philosophy.[2] The Australian military administrators seem to have had little conception of what the government of a large colonial territory entailed. Possibly this was a result of the lack of continuity caused by the succession of six administrators in less than seven years, though the fault was more likely to have been the limitations of the regime itself and of the men who ran it. As one scholar has noted, their appreciation of colonial problems was only that of the average patriotic layman: ' "native affairs" meant, in the main, matters relating to native labour with the emphasis on procurement and discipline . . . The native in his own village, minding his own business, did not receive much consideration, except as the object of taxation, or as a potential labourer'.[3] The Germans, on the other hand, had been working out a distinctive

63

colonial philosophy when war ended their rule. Under the guiding
hand of Dr Albert Hahl, the governor from 1903 to 1914 and an
official who has been described as 'the most successful of all German
colonial governors,[4] they had developed a colonial practice aimed
at protecting the New Guinean while bringing him into the European economy; they had devised the system of *luluais* and *tultuls* as
a solution to the problem of bringing large areas under control; they
were planning a vigorous medical policy and were about to embark
on an ambitious education programme; and, finally, they were encouraging villagers to grow cash crops.[5] Without a guiding
philosophy such as the Germans were able to bring to the problems
of rule, there was a lack of consistency in Australian administration.
This became apparent in many aspects of the Australian efforts in
the Lae region.

Lae was far from the centre of government—260 miles by sea
from the district office at Madang and 80 miles from the sub-district
headquarters at Morobe in the south of the Huon Gulf. In outposts
like Lae Australian policy was carried out through the periodical
visits of the District Officer or his assistants. The first such official
visit to Lae came in early 1915 when the new District Officer, Captain C. T. H. Nelson, toured the Gulf from Morobe to Finschhafen
to extract an oath of neutrality from each German in the region. This
tour resulted in a bad opening for mission-administration dealings.
Most of those taking the oath were missionaries and some demurred,
arousing Australian suspicions about their trustworthiness. Eventually three missionaries were interned in Australia, among them the
mission inspector Karl Steck, an important dignitary of the church
in Germany who was visiting the mission field when war broke out.
They were deported from New Guinea mainly because they refused
the oath, though there was also considerable mistrust for the role they
had played in the escape of Hermann Detzner, a German surveyor
who had refused to surrender when the Australians occupied
Morobe. With the help of some of the missionaries Detzner managed
to elude capture until the end of the war.[6] Events such as these
soured the relationship between the missionaries and the district
officials and their subsequent dealings were marked by mutual suspicion. To the credit of the Australians it must be said that their fear
of subversive mission influence was not entirely without foundation.
Though most missionaries were not interested in politics and signed
the oath readily enough, some remained ardent German nationalists
and even after the transfer of the colony to Australian civil adminis-

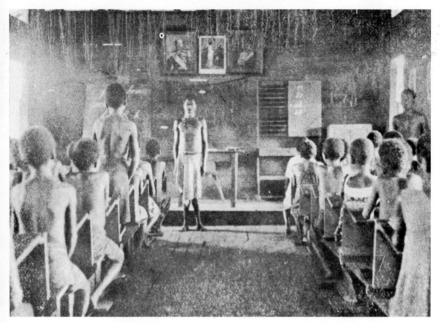

The Ampo mission school, about 1929

The *Bulolo* anchored off Voco Point, about 1940. The airstrip is far left and the Markham valley road runs inland towards the Atzera ranges.

Kahata Wakang, former paramount *Luluai* of Lae, and Butoawi, the only surviving children of Wakang, the first *Luluai* of Lae, 1973

Pastor Philemon Balob, the evangelist from Butibam who continued to conduct church services during World War II

Nagong Gejammec, who kept the Ampo School running during World War II

tration in 1921 they hoped it would eventually revert to German rule. They probably shared the attitude of the mission inspector, Steck, who shortly after the signing of the Mandate agreement in Versailles wrote in the mission newspaper, 'We hold the opinion that German New Guinea is German and is simply lost in foreign hands' then went on to say that 'Australian administration in no way compares with the German and few visitors have been able to express anything in favour of the businessmen and the administration in respect of their handling of the natives.'[7] Opinions such as these could hardly be expected to allay the suspicions of hostile Australians and ensured that the gulf between mission and government remained unbridged.

At first the Australians put Lae under the nominal care of the District Officer at Madang, but he controlled it so poorly that the Administrator, Brigadier-General Sir Samuel Pethebridge, transferred the responsibility to the Morobe office, noting that 'Madang has previously neglected this coast to such an extent that the natives recognise only one master—the missionaries.'[8] But once the neutrality of the missionaries was assured, the military administration took little interest in the local area except as a source of labour recruits: as one writer has noted, the missionaries 'were often disturbed by the illegal activities of the recruiters, but seldom by government visits'.[9] In dealing with the New Guinean community the missionaries had certain advantages over the officials. There were many more of them —eighty missionaries on twelve stations around the Gulf—than there were other whites, because only a handful of plantation owners, traders and *kiaps** lived in the district. The missionary spent all of his life in the one place with the same people, bringing them 'a positive message of hope, of fellowship in a world-wide brotherhood now and of eternal life hereafter'.[10] He therefore forged strong personal ties with local groups, whereas the government officer lived far away and arrived infrequently; consequently the people leaned towards the missionaries rather than the officials. This irritated the officials, who believed that they alone should have the loyalty of the people. The result of the mission-administration division was lax local control by the government, for without a large staff of *kiaps* the District Officers had to spread their resources thinly and they were not prepared to delegate their authority to the missionaries as the German officials had.

The *kiaps* had numerous duties. Much of their time was spent on

---

* I will continue to use the word *kiap* to describe the district officials because often the rank of particular officials is unknown.

the routine tasks that became the work pattern of patrol officers in later Australian administrations: they took censuses, examined village health, collected head tax and imposed labour duty, settled village disputes and apprehended wrongdoers, issued licences and collected licence fees; they checked the activities of *luluais* and *tultuls* and made appointments to these positions, conducted petty courts, built roads and worked on improving their station buildings, gardens and grounds.[11] However, few Australian patrol officers seem to have lived in Lae during the period of military rule, for the only recorded visits were those of Nelson in 1915, District Officer Jones and Corporal Hickley in 1917, and Lieutenant E. E. Jones, who lived there for five months in 1919 and built a substantial sub-district headquarters. Any patrolling therefore suffered by being too irregular or infrequent to have much lasting effect, and in practice the *kiap* generally arrived only after there had been major trouble. Thus the villagers could not have had a clear view of the intentions of the government. The *kiaps* must have appeared to them only as occasional interlopers who nevertheless had wide powers that could upset the normal routine of village life.

The *kiaps'* power to intervene in village affairs was demonstrated by several incidents during Lieutenant E. E. Jones's term of office in Lae in 1919. One of the *kiap's* duties was tax collection. At Lae Jones's first undertaking was a taxation patrol which collected £250 7s—even though 'the natives were very difficult to deal with. Did not seem to think it was really necessary to pay tax unless they wanted to'.[12] Previous patrols had apparently waived the tax or ignored it, with the result that Jones had to force it from the people. When he built his house at Lae he paid local villagers for the timber and sago thatch; he then collected as head tax the money he had just paid out. Apart from the irregularity of the collection of the tax and the various means used to extract it—cash, kind or labour—the people probably saw it as an elaborate ruse to separate them from their goods and cash or to make them work for nothing. Nevertheless, the insistence on the tax was probably important in educating them in the white man's economy. The German government had begun this lesson and the Australians continued it. Apparently it caused the people some hardship: from time to time Schmutterer saw fit to complain that 'the people have to drudge hard to pay their tax'.[13] He believed that the people received few benefits from their contributions. The *kiap's* role as a preserver of law and order was another aspect of his task that revealed his power over the lives of the people. At least one *kiap* had an exaggerated notion of his power here. After a village dispute near Sialum on the north coast of the Peninsula in March 1919 Jones 'threatened that if the fighting continued he would take a hand in it, and would not leave one man alive, and would burn their villages and destroy their gardens and the world would forget they ever existed'.[14] Then about a month later he harangued the people at Laukanu near Salamaua: 'I told them I would crush them if they did not obey me, making suitable actions to express my meaning. I finished up by reciting 'The Island Race'—of which not even the interpreter understood one single word—but it was most effective. Each headman gave me his weapons in token of his absolute and complete subjection'.[15]

One unfortunate result of the *kiaps'* playing God, as some were wont to do, was the effect on their subordinates, the police and the *luluais* and *tultuls*. There were many examples of overbearing, arrogant behaviour by the native officials. One such incident occurred at Labu, after the villagers complained that the police were molesting them. Jones promised that in future he would prevent this and deputed a policeman, Solom, to escort them back across the Markham. On reaching Labu, Solom fired a shot into one of the houses, as a result of which the Labu laid fresh charges before Jones. He informed them that the policeman would be sent to Morobe for punishment; but Solom let them know he would return later and burn down the village. For this he was given 'Field Punishment No. 1', that is he was suspended for a time by ropes attached to his wrists, then returned to Morobe for further punishment by the District Officer.[16] Further trouble came from the Butibam *luluai*, U., who had replaced the German appointee, Wakang, on the latter's death in 1917. The missionaries had trouble with his 'arbitrary behaviour' up until the time a patrol officer arrested him in 1918 on a charge of rape. The *kiap* 'gave him ten of the best in the village' and sent him to Morobe to face a charge before the District Officer, who dismissed him from service and gaoled him.[17] The problem with the native officials was that they modelled their own behaviour on the *kiaps'* overbearing ways. The right to hector villagers, interfere with their women and their goods was apparently taken to be a perquisite of office by many of the police and village officials. This damaged village-government relations because the people came to distrust both the *kiaps* and their native officials. Their suspicion of the government is seen in the assertion of one missionary that 'the people are becoming more perplexed because of the *kiap's* habit of pulling the wool over their eyes. The women and children now run off into the bush as soon as the conch shell warns of his approach'.[18]

Labour recruiting: the officials and recruiters versus the missionaries

The *kiaps'* main task in the Lae-Markham region was the super-vision of the labour trade. There had been a long history of recruiting around the Huon Gulf, dating back to the 1880s, but little in the Markham valley until its exploration after 1907 revealed thousands of inhabitants there. The Germans had only just begun tapping this potentially rich resource when war broke out. Full exploitation followed under the Australians. They took over the labour legisla-tion of the Germans, but although they made numerous modifica-tions to the German law the policy remained the same as under German rule at least until World War II: the utilization of the brute power of the New Guinean.[19]

World War I was a time of economic expansion for New Guinea. While prices for plantation products were rising, the German owners could not repatriate their funds and therefore reinvested in New Guinea. As a result the plantations expanded and the growth was soon apparent in increased demands for labour.[20] The coincidence of rising labour demands and the slackening of district control made for recruiting malpractices in remote corners such as the Markham. As the war continued the recruiters became more daring and recruiting abuses more blatant. One incident pointing to the boldness of the recruiters occurred at Malalo in April 1916. A man claiming to be a *kiap* arrived and after threatening the missionary with deportation, forcibly marched a large party of local men, including thirty-two schoolboys, aboard his launch. He later had engine trouble and called in at Finschhafen, where he dismissed his recruits, telling them to walk the eighty miles home. The missionaries contacted Rabaul and the man was arrested at Morobe on his way south into Papua. What punishment, if any, he received is unknown.[21] As the demand for labour increased similar incidents became more frequent around the Gulf and in the Markham. The *kiaps* chose to make a visit only after such events had taken place.

Despite the new interest the recruiters showed in the Markham valley, the coastal villages still provided a large quota of the labourers. In 1919, when the Lae village population was about 1700*, there were 192 villagers under contract, that is 11 per cent of the local population as against 9 per cent under the German regime in 1913. Recruiting was not only for plantations in New Guinea. The Germans had previously sent New Guineans to Nauru and Samoa and the Australians now continued this practice. Thus in 1916 a group of 98 men from the Huon Gulf—40 from Morobe, 50 from Garaina, 6 from Lae and 2 from Finschhafen—were sent to Nauru to dig phosphate for 9 years. The people seem not to have objected strenuously to the idea of recruitment and seem to have suffered the recruiters stoically. Labour service was the only means they had for accumulating much cash and those who wanted Western goods therefore had to engage for it. In addition some of the young men who signed up were probably looking for adventure and an escape from the routine and obligations of village life. Labour service was never an ideal occupation, however, because of the long period of absence required and because men often died while away. Half—49—of the group that went to Nauru in 1916 died there because of the unaccustomed hot, dry climate and the tiring work. There was thus a risk in volunteering as a recruit, because in every batch that went away there were some who never returned. The desertion rates of those recruited indicate that labour service was not highly popular: during the early period of civilian rule, from 1921 to 1926 (when such figures became available) as many as 11 per cent of the men who had been recruited in the Morobe District later deserted.

As the exodus of labourers mounted, the missionaries emerged as the champions of the village people, and the strongest advocates of strict controls over recruiting. They had an ambivalent attitude towards labour service, however. On the one hand Flierl, the founder of the mission, could boast that 'our mission has done much to make the natives willing to work for the white man'.[22] He also protested to the administration against the restriction of his power to mete out corporal punishment to labourers, calling on the scriptures for justification: 'The natives are mere children and some of them very naughty children . . . The Holy Scriptures say, Hebrews 12:7, For what son is he whom his father chastiseth not?'[23] The mission itself relied heavily on both day and contract labour to run many if its enterprises. By 1922 it was employing more than 330 contract

* This figure was a mission estimate which probably included the Labu Yalu, Tale and Tikeling in addition to the five Lae villages.

labourers alone, and therefore had an interest in seeing that the system of labour service continued. On the other hand it was Flierl who condemned the atrocities of the labour trade and reprimanded the government for failing to halt them. Throughout the period of military rule he and his colleagues petitioned the *kiaps* and administrators for better control of the recruiters. In May 1917 he advised the Administrator that he feared 'disturbances in the hinterland of the Huon Gulf and upper Markham River if the recruiting will be quite free without a close government control being provided'.[24] He requested the Administrator 'to close all new regions where the natives do not understand a contract for overseas recruiting.[25] The Administrator agreed, and banned recruiting for five miles on either side of the river above Munum.

But spasmodic visits by *kiaps* and the occasional closing of the Markham valley proved ineffectual means for controlling the trade. If closing the valley produced any effect at all, it merely diverted the trade to the heavily recruited coastal villages. After the valley had been closed for the second time, in 1917, one recruiter remarked, 'How can I know the closed territory when there are no posts around its boundary?'[26] Abuses of the trade became more frequent, and as trickery, threats, force and violence became more commonplace the Markham valley recruiters acquired a notorious reputation. There were numerous cases of impressment and the chaining and imprisonment of unwilling recruits, and on a number of occasions victims were beaten until they died. Violence was predictable because the recruiting parties went heavily armed. Often the recruiter sent his 'boys' out to hunt the prospects from surrounding villages. The consequences were perhaps predictable: gardens were plundered, houses looted, goods destroyed, women molested. Villages were often abandoned as the recruiters approached, the fitter young men escaping more quickly, with the result that the recruiters found only the women and old men. Sometimes the women were dragged off so that the men would offer themselves later. On one occasion some recruiters had locked a group of people inside a house and then set it alight. Flierl knew of nine cases where people had been shot, fourteen people dying as a result. In one incident near the Erap River in 1918, two Chinese and a Malay tried to take a group of young men forcibly. When they protested six were shot and six taken captive. The recruiters excused their action by asserting that they had acted in self defence. The recruiters' reign of terror cowed the people. When the District Officer eventually arrived, the missionaries took him through abandoned villages which the inhabitants had deserted to live in hiding in the bush. In other places the people were close to starvation because the recruiters had plundered and destroyed gardens. A great fear of the white man had been instilled into the people as a result. One of the missionaries wrote that in the villages 'fear of the Bumbum*, the Kongong* and the Malay is the most common theme of talking'.[27] When he exhorted them, 'You must not fear sorcery and ghosts', their answer generally was, 'No, we fear Bumbum'.[28]

The government was forced to take action when it learnt, from the missionaries, what was happening. In October 1918 when the Administrator, Brigadier-General J. G. Johnston, received a long treatise on the Markham labour trade from Flierl, he was shocked and complimented the missionary on 'disclosing a state of affairs which is a disgrace to civilization'.[29] He instituted an enquiry by sending the District Officer to investigate. This official subsequently reported that it was impossible to identify those guilty of illegal actions because most of the abuses had been committed by unknown New Guinean recruiters; furthermore, much of the evidence was hearsay and the witnesses were 'wild, savage and unreliable', and it would be impossible to collect them together for a court hearing against the guilty recruiters.[30] The Administrator concluded that the abuses had undoubtedly taken place, but because of the practical difficulties of prosecuting the guilty parties, the only action he felt he could take was to cancel the licences of the recruiters who were under suspicion, and to post a *kiap* at Lae temporarily to control the trade.

Lae, as well as being a source of recruits, was important to the recruiters as a base camp for their inland activities. They also used men from Lae as assistants on their expeditions. There was profit in the trade for the coastal men who accompanied such patrols, as the wages were good. They were not always willing to go with the recruiters, however, because they knew it could lead to trouble with both mission and government. The recruiters sometimes forced the demurrers. One Malay recruiter arrived at Lae seeking assistants for a trip up the Markham on behalf of the Neu Guinea Compagnie. The *luluai* was reluctant to help in rounding up a team because the Malay had no authority from the District Officer. The recruiter then 'spoke strong' at the men of the village and offered them various sums up to eight shillings—nearly two months' pay—to go with him.

* *Bumbum* is the Yabem word for white man and *Kongkong* the Pidgin word for Chinese.

Eventually about five of them, including the *luluai* and *tultul*, gave in. On the first night out of Lae they linked up with a Chinese recruiter who was also working for the Compagnie. The combined party moved up the valley to Guruf and while the Malay and Chinese waited in the village their coastal assistants went off armed and under the guidance of the Guruf evangelist, who had been persuaded to help 'bring in the kanakas'.[31] They succeeded in capturing six men and were marching them off tied together when a group of the captives' friends attacked. The captives broke free, and the recruiters were driven down to the Markham, which they had to swim to escape.

The action of the *kiap* on hearing of this incident demonstrates the ineffectiveness of the government in such situations where insufficient trained and dedicated staff were available for effective district control. When the *kiap*, Jones, heard what had happened he wrote to Helmut Baum, a German recruiter also at work in the Markham, instructing him to bring in the Malay and the Chinese for illegal recruiting. He was thus using methods that were just as open to abuse as the recruiting system itself, for his delegation of authority to Baum was irregular and led to further trouble. When Baum returned from the Markham, he complained that nine recruits had engaged but had run away after accepting his trade goods. Jones then sent out two native policemen to find the goods and the labourers. They recovered the goods from a *luluai* but reported that they were unable to find the men because they had been attacked. He later discovered from Lehner that they had been attacked for seducing a village woman. This news enraged him, because he recognized it as a distinct set-back to his task in the Markham. He packed the two policemen back to Morobe for punishment by the District Officer, asking that 'the sentences should be such as would deter the police from further interference with the kanakas'.[32]

Because of incidents like these, the missionaries carefully scrutinized the activities of the recruiters and government officials, using their network of evangelists to keep them advised of what was happening on the outstations. Lehner, in fulminating against what he believed was 'slave trading in modern garb', expressed this hope: 'May the evangelists be steadfast men! May they prove to be a thorn in the eyes of the traders!'[33] For their part the recruiters resented what they believed was the missionaries' unwarranted interference in their business. The owner of Singaua plantation east of Lae, H. Andexer (who was a renowned recruiter), showed this when he threatened to prosecute Flierl 'on account of insults' the missionary was supposed to have made about him in correspondence with the Administrator.[34] The Australian *kiaps* generally agreed that recruiting was no concern of the missionaries. They recognized that the missionaries had an ambivalent attitude to the labour trade and despised them for it. They regarded the intervention of the mission as a nuisance, and informed their superiors in Rabaul that the missionaries had a vested interest in the trade, and were interested in the people only in so far as they were left without competition for their services. The attitude of the *kiaps* was well summed-up by the Morobe District Officer in 1917. After Flierl had made representations to the Administrator about the spread of epidemics, foods shortages, tax collection, and the labour trade, he wrote a long complaint to Rabaul stating that the missionary was 'reporting on work which has nothing to do with him'.[35] He interpreted this as an insult to my ability and fairness as a British Officer. I feel sure I can be relied on to act with as much and more fairness than any German missionary'.[36] He went on to take the side of the recruiters against the missionaries, asserting that

> the planters have great difficulty in getting labour from the coast. The missionaries are hard taskmasters and get a lot for very little pay. At Lae the missionary gets the men of his village to come from time to time to his station to make gardens for the upkeep of the school-children. These people get no pay for this and I would like to ask Your Excellency if they should be paid as day labourers'.[37]

Given the attitudes of the *kiaps*, the planters and the traders, it was perhaps inevitable that they should unite against the missionaries. A number of them appear to have struck up close friendships. Isolated from the company of other whites, of whom there were few around the Gulf, the *kiaps* probably found the recruiters and planters more to their taste than the missionaries. Jones, for example, became a close friend of Andexer, to whom he paid this back-handed compliment: 'Andexer was like a dead German, that is he was a good German. When I was ill with fever on patrol from Morobe he never left me for three days and nights. I am convinced that had it not been for Andexer I would not now be writing'.[38] As a result of such personal bonds, the *kiaps* were predisposed towards the recruiters in any dispute with the missionaries. They were intensely prejudiced against the missionaries, whom they regarded as subversive, and they believed they had a sacred duty to undermine their influence among the local people. They therefore took perverse delight in obstructing and baiting the missionaries at every opportunity. How serious the animosity was between the *kiaps* and missionaries was possibly not known to the central government. At least one Administrator, Johnston, appreciated the efforts of the missionaries to protect the villagers from illegal recruiting: he once wrote to Flierl, 'I quite appreciate the motive which activated your complaints and thank you most sincerely for bringing them to my notice'.[39] However, at the local level the *kiaps* did not share this attitude, and Flierl saw cause to point out to the Administrator that he would be unable to realise his hopes of ending recruiting malpractices if his *kiaps* did not share his 'high ideals and good principles'.[40]

There were numerous instances of the malice of the local Australian officials. In January 1919 the District Officer convened an enquiry into allegations Lehner had made about improper recruiting methods in the Markham. It was conducted at Singaua, against whose proprietors, Andexer and Merseburger, the charges had been made. The District Officer sided with the planters and used his enquiry as an opportunity for sniping at the missionary, thereby discrediting him before his congregation. Lehner responded in kind, preaching his next sermon against the 'dung beetles and mouths of dogs' as he called those who had spoken against him.[41] He was clearly able to give as good as he received. Not so fortunate was Stürzenhofecker, the missionary in charge of Malahang plantation, whom Jones fined £5 for 'gross and callous neglect' of the health of one of his contract labourers. Jones had been waging a petty feud with Stürzenhofecker and after convicting him wrote jubilantly to the District Officer, 'What do you think of the charge against Stuffeneck? Hope you will confirm it. Never saw a man so wild in all my life and have not had a pleasant a half hour since I came up here'.[42]

The effects of incidents such as these was not lost on the local people, who could see, perhaps for the first time, that the missionaries were not impregnable and that they did not possess incontrovertible authority. Those who may have had a grudge against a particular missionary—the villagers who informed on Lehner during the Singaua enquiry, the labourer who reported Stürzenhofecker to Jones—realized that when a temporal authority existed in opposition to the spiritual, the one could be successfully played off against the other. There were numerous cases where villagers attempted to do this. One one occasion the Labu *tultul*, H., who was unhappily married, seduced his brother's fiancée. The girl moved into his house when the brother went away to work. Realizing that the congregation and mission would probably exclude him, H. attempted to forestall this by going to the *kiap* complaining that his wife was jealous, mean and disobedient and that he wanted to divorce her; because he was a *tultul* he received a sympathetic hearing. He then went to the missionary, confessed that he had sinned, and begged for forgiveness. He now returned to the village and said he had the approval of both the *kiap* and the missionary. His gambit was unsuccessful, however, for when the congregation discovered what had happened he was excommunicated.[43] Another one who attempted to play government and mission off together was U., the *luluai* deposed for rape. After his appointment he set himself against the authority of the mission by advising the men of the village to ignore the mission's ruling on polygamy and to take additional wives. He also went out of his way to interfere in congregational decisions in an effort to disrupt Schmutterer's influence.[44] The existence of a temporal power which saw itself as a competitor of the mission gave such people as U. immunity from the disapprobation of the missionaries and from censure by the congregation. The result for the villagers was the erosion of the monopoly of authority in village affairs which had been carefully fostered by the mission and the congregational elders.

The opposing moral standards of the missionaries and non-mission whites was also important in reducing the influence of the mission. The *kiaps*, recruiters and planters, and later the agricultural officers and road construction supervisors of the civilian administration, showed the people a facet of European life they had not seen before. Until later in the period of military rule most of the white men coming to Lae were missionaries, to whose regular, abstemious and puritanical life style the people had become accustomed. It appeared that the missionaries' code was the norm for Europeans, yet non-mission whites tended to live according to different moral standards. A number of them made a habit of sleeping with village women while on patrol, and on one occasion a *kiap* who was staying with Friederich Bayer, the Malalo missionary, kept a girl with him in the mission house, to the consternation of the missionary and in full view of the local villagers, who were amazed that such things could be. The intrusion of a rival set of moral values proved disruptive. The case of K., a Labu evangelist, illustrates something of the tensions caused by conflicting moral codes. K. became engaged to a Labu girl who was coveted by one of the *kiaps*. He was therefore removed from the scene by a six month gaol sentence in Morobe, and in his absence the official took the girl.[45] A similar incident involved a member of the Tikeling congregation who was excommunicated when he began living with a woman he was not married to. The *kiaps* heard about it and gaoled him for several months for adultery; in the meantime 'the evil woman served the whites'.[46] When her brother tried to intervene and bring her back to the village he received a month's gaol for his trouble. Those who remained loyal to the old morality and the values of the congregation could thus expect to be treated as common transgressors if they stood in the way of the *kiaps*.

The feuding between the missionaries and the officials and their contrary moral values were important in eroding the influence of the mission. However, the *kiaps* did not leave it to chance but actively worked to see that this happened. They took every opportunity to best the missionaries and wean the loyalty of the people from them. These aims could be seen in a huge *singsing** which Jones, the Assistant District Officer, staged at Lae in 1919 as the culmination of his tour of duty there. The purpose of this celebration was 'to gain the confidence of the Markham valley natives who were pleased to have the security of the station at Lae, but too timid to come to Lae to meet the *kiap*'.[47] Nearly three thousand people came from thirty-four villages as far apart as the mountains behind Salamaua, the Buang hills behind Labu, and the far reaches of the Waing and upper Markham. The Bukaua were supposed to come too, but did not turn up, possibly because Lehner had discouraged them from attending. Lehner had wanted to use the meeting for a mass church service of the combined congregations, along the lines of the mission's *Sam* festival. But Jones would not agree to this because he wished to outshine the mission and wanted no competition from that source. The *singsing* was a vast undertaking: Jones purchased 3000 lbs of taro, nine pigs, a roll of calico and 15 lbs of tobacco as food and presents for those attending. He used the occasion to meet remote villagers he had not visited, and to appoint *luluais* and *tultuls* among them. Except for one case of rape, which he punished by beating the offender in public and then sentencing him to six months' gaol, the meeting went off without incident and he was pleased to note that the people 'quickly gained confidence and appeared both surprised

---

* *Singsing* is Pidgin for celebration or festivity, usually involving singing, dancing and feasting.

and pleased with the arrangements I had made for their comfort and safety'.[48] He had thus proved to them that, like the mission, the government could gather many different peoples from all over the district and assist them to meet in peace; this had been one of the main achievements of the mission's *Sam* festival. He had also shown them that the government could provide for them on such occasions, just as well as the mission did. Whether or not the people saw that the government was offering itself as a serious competitor for their loyalty is not clear, but if they could the effect was probably to weaken the influence of the mission and the traditional values it stood for.

The civilian regime

The civilian government, which took control of New Guinea in May 1921, provided continuity with the former military regime. This was facilitated by the retention in the civilian service of many officials of the military administration. Many of the policies and practices of the new were indistinguishable from those of the old, particularly with regard to native labour, health, education and taxation. Patrolling also resembled the practice of earlier periods as it continued to be irregular and spasmodic. The first patrol of the civilian regime through Lae did not take place until 1923–4 when the District Officer, Ted Taylor, a *kiap* retained from the military regime, and a patrol officer, George Ellis, went into the Markham. They were pleased to find 'the natives to be friendly and peacefully disposed . . . and as a rule intelligent and capable of being trained'.[49] Though they were blissfully unaware of the years of work done in the area by the missionaries, the German officials, and the *kiaps* of the Australian regime, they made a thorough patrol: they censused 41 167 people in the region, the total population of which was estimated at 68 000 and reported that 'every village and hamlet was visited'.[50] Lae was also graced from time to time by the arrival of higher dignitaries. In 1925 the Administrator, Major-General E. A. Wisdom, came to inspect the newly commenced Markham valley road. He visited local villages and met the *luluais* and *tultuls*, 'affording them every opportunity of ventilating grievances, preferring requests and bringing under his notice their views on various matters'.[51] Such visits, however, like those of the German and military administrators in an earlier era, were too infrequent and formal to have had any great effect on the villagers, except perhaps by striking awe of the government into them.

The most significant step the new government took in the Markham was the opening of permanent agricultural stations at Lae and at Sangan in the upper Markham. The post at Lae was established in 1925 when the Department of Agriculture set up a plant nursery under the control of a European supervisor. The purpose of this was twofold: it was the coastal base for the experimental farm at Sangan and the depot from which the Markham valley road was to be built. The government considered the Markham had great potential for development and therefore wanted a road in as quickly as possible. Many crops were tried at Sangan (maize, peanuts, castor oil, kapok, coffee, cotton and rice) of which cotton had the greatest potential and samples worth 18d per lb, a very good price at the time, were grown there. Despite its promise the Sangan station was closed in 1929, a victim of the inertia of the Great Depression and also of 'staff trouble' which involved the European agricultural officers interfering with the local women and antagonizing the local men by doing so. When Sangan closed Lae was retained to produce vegetables for the native labourers employed on the construction of the Markham road and, later, for the government workforce at the new district headquarters at Salamaua. The officer in charge of both the agricultural station at Lae and the road building programme was Tommy Wright, who was something of a New Guinea identity and a man typical of the itinerant Europeans who drifted into the Morobe District during the 1920s and 30s. He had grown up in Port Moresby, where his mother ran a guest house, and had worked as recruiter, supervisor of native labour and general handyman on construction jobs. During 1925–6 Wright pushed on energetically with the construction of the road, through the thick coastal rainforest to a point about fourteen miles inland, with the aim of linking Lae with Gabsonkek, twenty miles away. In 1927–28, however, the task was transferred to the Public Works Department and little more was done, mainly because the establishment of air transport obviated the need for a road.[52]

The foundation of the agricultural station and road construction camp at Lae was an important event for the local villagers. Not only did it give them work, it also brought into the area for the first time large numbers of outside workers. Since 1916, of course, the Malahang plantation had been gathering numbers of workers together, but these tended to come from local villages and were therefore under the control of the mission and the congregation. Wright's workforce, however, was a large secular body of more than two hundred men drawn from a wide area around the Gulf and beyond. It was a body that came under the jurisdiction of neither mission nor congregation and its members were not integrated into the mission-congregation system of social control and were unbound by the limitations and obligations this imposed on the villagers. It thus offered the people an alternative system of behaviour to that permitted by mission and congregation and presented them with possibilities for independent action which the villagers did not enjoy under the traditional system reinforced by the mission. For these reasons it acted as a disruptive influence on the close-knit village community and church congregation. Villagers who resented the restrictions of life in the congregation could now escape by joining the secular workforce. This could only serve to erode the authority and control of the mission and congregation. Schmutterer indicated what was happening when he wrote that the 'station close by remains a temptation and not only for the men. I have pupils in my school whose highest ideal is to run around with the station people'.[53] Wright's agricultural station was working as a magnet, drawing the young people away from the strictly-ordered life of the village and congregation. A frequent complaint was now heard: 'The young people do not care. The congregational elders protest, "What shall we do? We give them punishments, we exclude them from the villages and all this is no use" '.[54] The youths were becoming dissatisfied with the restraints of the village society and were beginning to break away.

The years of military and early civilian rule were an important period for the villagers around Lae. Although they had been confirmed in their allegiance to Christianity and the mission had expanded around them, the non-mission whites and the Australian *kiaps* had sown seeds of dissatisfaction among them. Heavy pressures were brought to bear upon them to change their loyalties. Mission influence and the village-congregation synthesis were weakning. A new synthesis was therefore needed.

5

THE GROWTH OF A TOWN

Apart from Tommy Wright's agricultural station and Gottfried Schmutterer's mission station at Ampo on the far side of the Bumbu, there was no permanent European settlement at Lae until the construction of the aerodrome in 1927. After that a town grew rapidly, and it eventually became the capital of New Guinea in the final months before the outbreak of war in the Pacific. As the town expanded it developed a separate life of its own which could exist without reference to the villages around it. Lae grew not so much as a town within its own rights but as an integral part of an interdependent group of towns built for the exploitation of the Morobe District goldfields, and was important as the hub of the aviation system linking Salamaua, Bulolo, Wau and Edie Creek.

The aerodrome and the aviation service

The discovery of gold at Edie Creek above Wau in 1926 sparked off a gold rush which led to the exploitation of the rich deposits of the Bulolo-Watut river system by large-scale mechanized mining. The rigours and cost of the eight-day walk into the goldfields and the difficulty of building a road from the coast led to the early introduction of an aviation service.[1] The driving force behind the development of the goldfields was Cecil J. Levien, a former Morobe District Officer who has been described as a 'rare and formidable combination of opportunist, practical man and visionary'.[2] Levien persuaded the directors of Guinea Gold N.L. that startling profits would be made by any aviation company that could provide a service to eliminate the arduous walk between Salamaua and Wau. He secured an option on a small DH-37 plane in Melbourne and engaged a pilot, E. A. ('Pard') Mustar, to bring it to New Guinea. He then selected Lae as the best place for the coastal airstrip, and without bothering to obtain official permission took on about two hundred and fifty labourers to clear and level a landing ground under the supervision of Tommy Wright, the foreman of the agricultural station.

The construction of the airfield was perhaps the biggest enterprise ever undertaken at Lae and greatly perturbed the local villagers, who watched amazed as a vast area of bush was torn down and gardens were flattened. They were in for further surprises when Mustar and his mechanic, A. W. D. Mullins, flew in from Rabaul, where they had been assembling and testing the plane. Their arrival brought the full power of Western technology home to the villagers with a shock. Mustar's account of his landing in Lae on 30 March 1927 gives a sharp sense of their mixed excitement and confusion:

> Our staff welcomed the machine . . . And the Kanakas! Good Lord! They came in droves to see the 'big feller pidgeon'. My engineer, Mullins, was over six feet tall, while I am only 5ft. 6ins. short, and the Kanakas couldn't understand why the little man was 'Number one masta longa pidgeon'. They examined the machine and decided it was 'strong feller too much. Me no savvy this feller fashion belong white master'. Some of these natives had travelled for days down the mountains to see the 'pidgeon' . . . They took full measurements of the wings and all parts of the machine with lengths of cane to carry back to wondering villagers.[3]

The mastery of Europeans, previously seen in their goods and possessions, was now indisputable.

The aviation service was a success from the start. After two unsuccessful flights around the mountains south of the Markham—no one knew exactly how to find Wau from the air—Mustar landed at Wau for the first time on 16 April. He began the service the next day with a shipment of six 100 lb bags of rice, charging a shilling a lb, and, making two trips a day, five days a week, carried 84 passengers and 27 000 lbs of cargo in the first three months. Rival aviation companies were not long in arriving to share the profits. Ray Parer, the proprietor of Bulolo Goldfields Air Service who had been competing keenly with Mustar to be the first to land at Lae, came from Rabaul after many delays, and A. ('Jerry') Pentland and P. ('Skip') Moody soon joined them. There was ample business for all, and by April 1928, a year after the service began, Guinea Airways (the aviation company that grew from Guinea Gold N.L.) had acquired two extra planes and was employing three further pilots and two more mechanics. Then in March 1929 a new company, Morlae Airlines, began a weekly Lae–Port Moresby run, meeting ships from Australia and bringing passengers and frozen foods across to Wau, Bulolo, Salamaua and Lae. This service cut the time needed to get from Port Moresby to the goldfields from six days to one.[4]

The town developed quickly as the volume of traffic increased. What had been a rough clearing in the bush in early 1927 soon acquired workshops, hangars, storage sheds, offices, houses and barracks. At first the growth was unsupervised and chaotic. Guinea Gold N.L. had built the airstrip without permission and had no power to prevent other operators from using the land or erecting buildings. As a result early Lae grew as a large European squatter camp. Each new arrival simply set himself up wherever he pleased without concern for ownership. Levien in particular was concerned at the uncontrolled building, which he believed was becoming a hazard to aircraft.[5] No one was sure who owned the land, but that the local villagers may have had rightful claims does not seem to have been considered.

The question of ownership was finally settled in favour of the administration. The government, with might on its side, ended the squabbling between the various contenders by resuming a large area including the airstrip in August 1927. Earlier the land had been put up for sale by tender by the Custodian of Expropriated Properties, who had control of it because it was the property that had been expropriated from the Neu Guinea Compagnie. The administration had been a tenderer, but concerned that it might be outbid by an ambitious, go-getting company like Guinea Gold N.L., it withdrew its tender and resumed the land instead. The government took a huge slice—the entire 11 721 acres of the Compagnie's holding— stating that it needed the land for an aerodrome, a shipping depot, an agricultural station, and native reserves.[6] Those wanting to build now had to arrange a lease with the government. The administration was strongly influenced by an officer of the Department of Civil Aviation, W. J. Duncan, who had been seconded by the Australian government to the New Guinea administration to report on and supervize the founding of aviation services in New Guinea. Duncan's report, which he submitted in late 1927, recommended that the administration should take responsibility for airport construction and maintenance, that it should sub-divide the area around the airstrip into a series of blocks, each three chains wide and five chains long with a roadway between them and lease each for £20 a year.[7]

Lae thus became the prototype for New Guinean towns built around airstrips. In such places the airstrip dominates the shape and form of the town, usually occupying the central position. (Later airport towns were Goroka, Mount Hagen, Kainantu and most sub-district headquarters opened since World War II.) The airstrip in New Guinea is perhaps analogous to the railway station of an earlier era in America and Australia, because it has generally decided the shape and the settlement pattern of the town. In early Lae this was obvious: the workshops and hangars clustered between the end of the airstrip and the wharf, the Europeans lived to the east of the strip, near the river terrace, while the New Guinean labourers generally lived on the far, or western side.

An important impetus to the growth of Lae was the decision of the gold mining interests to airlift in sections the heavy mining machinery they used for treating the Bulolo and Watut River gravels. At first Bulolo Gold Dredging Ltd and its parent company, Placer Development Ltd, had thought of building a road to the goldfields, but the length of time it would take and the high cost of construction and maintenance persuaded the companies to accept Guinea Airways' proposition that 'skyways are the cheapest highways'.[8] On the advice of Mustar, Bulolo Gold Dredging purchasel three all-metal, tri-motored Junkers G-31 aircraft from Germany, which Guinea Airways was to operate under licence for the gold mining company; Guinea Airways also purchased a Junkers G-31 of its own. They were huge planes, each capable of carrying a payload of 7100 lbs, or 14 short tons together. The airlift began in April 1931 and continued for eight years: the first dredge began work in March 1932, the eighth in November 1939. It proceeded smoothly because of the spirit of co-operation existing between Bulolo Gold Dredging and Guinea Airways, and because of their streamlined operation. At Lae they had a wharf 75 feet long, with half a mile of railway running around the foreshore to the storage sheds at the airport. Because of the unsatisfactory harbour facilities at Lae—unstable foreshore, open anchorage and steeply sloping seafloor—all cargo had to be lightered ashore in barges, which were then unloaded by steam crane. Another crane at the airstrip lifted the heavy machinery into the planes and a rail crane unloaded them at Bulolo. Eventually operations became so efficient that nine round trips a day were possible. The airlift was a remarkable undertaking. It pioneered the use of aviation in the transport of heavy cargo and, in the words of one writer, 'in every respect it constituted a world record'.[9] While it lasted the power of

Western technology was daily impressed on the local people, who stood by bemused as the town grew around them.

The airlift stimulated the steady development of the town and by 1942, when it was destroyed by Japanese bombing, it had about 120 European residents, about sixty Chinese and perhaps several hundred New Guineans. It became a bustling, busy place, and though it remained chiefly a centre of the aviation industry, it developed a distinctive town life of its own. Something of its busyness can be seen in a 1935 report in the *Pacific Islands Monthly*:

> Lae is now a township ranking high in the Mandated Territory of New Guinea. It is a centre of great activity . . . and one of the biggest (if not the biggest) aircraft centres in the southern hemisphere. The European population is now around the hundred mark and is increasing with each steamer. Accommodation is being taxed; so much so that a new hotel has been commenced and is expected to be completed in a month or two.[10]

Lae and Salamau

Because Lae grew as a 'company' town, the headquarters of the aviation companies, it had a number of deficiencies. Most of its inhabitants were young single men or men who had left their families in Australia. This was reflected in the goldfields social life: in August 1929 when the first dance was organized at Wau, all the women from Salamaua, Wau and Lae attended, a total of twelve. Lae was thus a work camp for males and had no school, no church and no hospital. Those who were ill went to the hospital at Salamaua, and those who wanted spiritual consolation but were not prepared to attend the Yabem services at Ampo had to wait for the occasional visits of the Anglican vicar from Wau. Guinea Airways employed its own medical orderlies, but the standards of service were poor. One of the medical orderlies, Bill Edwards, who also doubled as the sanitary contractor, road foreman and recruiter, used to cook his food in the sterilizer. The manageress of the hotel blamed him for her blood poisoning after he gave her an injection with a needle sterilized in the sausage water. The usual remedy for any New Guinean suffering from bodily tinea (Pidgin: *grili*)—an unsightly affliction bringing social isolation—was a liberal coating of caustic diesel oil applied with a paintbrush. And the whites of the town were amused once when a labourer's arm had been broken, and the orderly had mistakenly set the hand in the reverse position. Occasionally the lack of medical facilities at Lae caused a crisis, as in 1928 when one of the pilots, Bill Wiltshire, fell dangerously ill with a liver abscess. The doctor had to be called urgently from Salamaua, and because Salamaua had no airstrip at the time, another of the Lae pilots, Alan Cross, flew over and 'dive-bombed' his house with notes asking him to come at once in the government launch. Pre-war New Guinea was an unpleasant place for whites because it was unhealthy: one resident of early Lae recalls that he had malaria twenty-five times and dengue fever three times in three years. The whites who came to Lae were thus generally reluctant residents, afraid of the diseases they would catch there. For this reason they formed no permanent attachment to the place or the people and instead they looked forward to their departure.

The Europeans of Lae had to put up with many unaccustomed hardships, one of which was the lack of shops. After 1930 a number of trade stores were established, mainly by Chinese, but these catered for the needs of the New Guinean labourers rather than for the European community. The first storekeeper was Henry Eekhoff, who had originally come to Lae to take over the government agricultural station. When the station closed down in 1930 he opened a trade store, ran a guest house and sold beer. He was eminently successful in drawing the native trade away from his Chinese competitors, who could not understand that his success came from hiding a shilling piece in every hundredth one pound pack of rice he sold. He later sold his guest house and beer licence to Mrs Flora Stewart, the owner of the Wau hotel and a renowned New Guinea identity who had run a hotel in Samarai and had been on the Sapphire Creek copper mining field in Papua before coming to the goldfields. It was 'Ma' Stewart who built the town's first hotel. Burns Philp opened a branch of their Salamaua store at Lae in 1930 to facilitate the movement of frozen foods between Salamaua and the goldfields, but it sold only meat and the most essential groceries. Europeans therefore had to rely heavily on Salamaua for many of their needs. Guinea Airways recognized this and allowed the wives of staff to travel across to Salamaua on the company's launch for a day's shopping once a week. The women enjoyed this day in town as a social occasion, as did any of the men who had to go across for medical or dental treatment. The trip over was leisurely and relaxing and the bustle of Salamaua made a welcome change from the monotony of Lae.

Gradually the rough living conditions improved. From the early days electric power had been supplied by the Guinea Airways generator, and the company continued to provide this service. A post office, situated in the Guinea Airways offices and manned by a company clerk, opened in 1932. There were no banks until the Bank of New South Wales and the Commonwealth Bank opened in Lae in 1941; before that all banking was done at Salamaua. The regular supply of fresh dairy, poultry and garden produce, from the Lutheran mission at Ampo and from Malahang plantation, and later from Bob Emery's Balumbia plantation and Carl Jacobsen's poultry farm*, was welcome. A further well-received addition was the creation of a regular airmail link with Australia in 1934. It was then possible at least once a week to read that morning's Brisbane newspaper. 'Ma' Stewart's Hotel Cecil, completed in March 1936, was perhaps the town's most popular amenity with the whites. The Lae correspondent of the *Pacific Islands Monthly* proudly described it thus:

> It is a well constructed modern building with a comfortable sitting room on the ground floor and has plenty of bathrooms and running water. The commodious bar and billiards room are up-to-date and the kitchen is remarkable for its size and conveniences. The bedrooms are large and airy. A verandah runs around the top floor, well shaded and made comfortable by lounge chairs and small tables.[11]

The Cecil was the scene of many gay parties, dinners and balls which allowed the white residents to forget they were far from home. On such occasions they observed the social niceties punctiliously and the local correspondents of the *Rabaul Times* and the *Pacific Islands Monthly* fondly dwelt on the minutiae of each social event. At one of the first parties, for example, he observed that

> everyone enjoyed the dancing . . . Mrs Chater in mauve satin was here, there and everywhere. Mrs Ross in flowered morocain was noticed as was also Mrs Gething in royal blue and crepe. Others present were Mrs Baldie in tomato red lace, Mrs Johnson in blue organdie, Mrs Priebe in figured morocain with cowl neck, and Mrs Balfour in pink organdie[12];

and then after the fancy dress ball of October 1936 he proudly reported that 'the costumes were of the highest standards and would rival the Artists' Ball of southern climes'.[13] Gradually life became

---

* Emery's plantation occupied the site of the present Botanical Gardens. Jacobsen's property was on the site of the present golf course.

more tolerable in Lae and as it did a number of European and Chinese residents put down roots and began making their permanent homes in the town.

Despite the growth of its amenities Lae remained but a 'company' town and was very much a satellite of Salamaua. Salamaua sprang up before Lae and because it was the administrative and commercial centre of the district and also the port for the goldfields it continued to dominate its sister across the Gulf right up till World War II. The shipping interests refused to accept Lae as a port, probably because they had already established themselves at Salamaua before Lae developed. The trading firms and administration depended on shipping rather than aviation and chose to build at the port most convenient to the shipping companies. Lae's growth was also hampered by rivalry between the powerful New Guinea Goldfields Ltd and Guinea Airways. Because of disputes with the aviation firm New Guinea Goldfields, the mining company based on Wau, sponsored the building of the Salamaua airstrip and had purchased its own plane in 1929 as a means of minimizing its dependence on Guinea Airways.[14] Once Salamaua had its own aerodrome and aviation companies there was a direct link with the goldfields which bypassed Lae. The administration and commercial firms now had no need to rely on Guinea Airways and could operate easily out of Salamaua. As a result Salamaua remained the main town of the goldfields complex.

The government, like the shipping companies, actively resisted pressures to have Lae built up as the chief town of the Morobe District. The district headquarters had been moved up from Morobe to Salamaua in 1926 and once ensconced there the administration was not interested in moving again. At times it even affirmed its preference for Salamaua by stubbornly refusing to use either the aviation or shipping facilities at Lae. On one occasion the Administrator, while on an urgent flight to Australia, preferred a day's delay at Salamaua rather than to fly on a plane routed through Lae.[15] Except for visits from the District Officer and members of his staff and occasional inspections by the Administrators and Commonwealth ministers, the residents of Lae were left much to their own devices until September 1935 when an Assistant District Officer, Alan Roberts, arrived to open a sub-district office. By this time it was necessary for the government to have a man permanently in Lae. The European population had passed the one hundred mark and a regular air link had been established with Australia, so that a per-

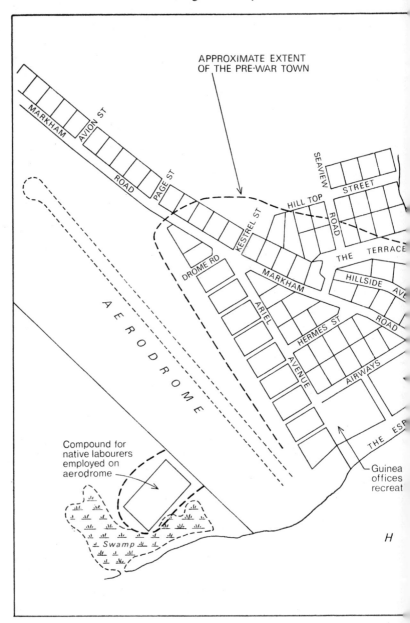

The first town plan of Lae, 1938

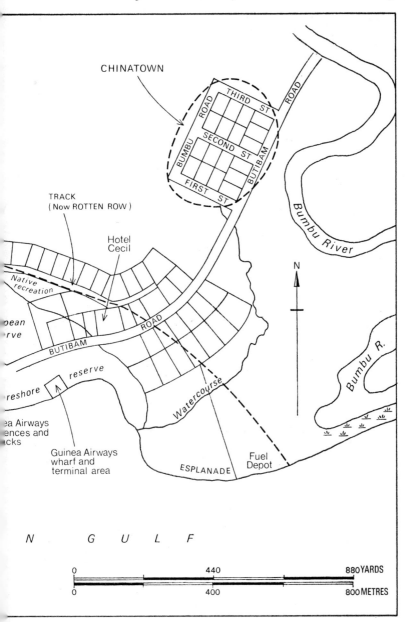

CHINATOWN

THIRD ST

SECOND ST

FIRST ST

BUMBU ROAD

BUTIBAM ROAD

ROAD

Bumbu River

Bumbu R.

TRACK
(Now ROTTEN ROW)

Hotel
Cecil

Native
recreation

pean
rve

BUTIBAM ROAD

reshore reserve

a Airways
ences and
cks

Guinea Airways
wharf and
terminal area

Watercourse

N

ESPLANADE

Fuel
Depot

N   G   U   L   F

| 0 | 440 | 880 YARDS |
| 0 | 400 | 800 METRES |

manent customs post was necessary. Roberts had a staff of two—a patrol officer and a customs clerk—and a squad of police. His main duties were the supervision of the post office, the collection of customs duties, and patrolling the sub-district, the boundaries of which were the Markham to the west, the Waing and Momolili regions to the north and northeast, and Bukaua to the east.

The social life of Lae

Lae was a hard-playing, hard-drinking town with a boisterous social life revolving around the Hotel Cecil and the Guinea Airways recreation club. The club's flood-lit tennis courts, concrete swimming pool, cricket ground, piano, billiards table, and regular cinema-shows were popular attractions for the Europeans. With a population of mainly young single men, many of the entertainments were high-spirited. After the Easter swimming carnival in 1936, for example, 'the competitors turned their attention to the onlookers. It is apparently an old Lae custom', the *Rabaul Times* noted, 'that when the competitions are over all the onlookers are thrown into the pool. One can imagine the scamper when the onlooking youths dashed wildly in any direction pursued by yelling friends clad only in bathers'.[16] Drinking was one of the main pastimes and many social events were notable for the amount of liquor consumed. In 1936 the *Rabaul Times* described one of Lae's parties, a farewell for the pilot Orme Denny:

> The boys decided to say goodbye to their friend in the good old usual way. Until the early hours of the morning one could hear guitars strumming and many voices lifted to the tune of 'For he's a jolly good fellow' at various intervals. The wine flowed freely and glad were the hearts of all. What matter if the cold light of morning brings rain, regrets and a blinding headache while there is still a day's work to be done.[17]

What impression such horse-play and carousing made on the New Guinean community is not clear, though they probably understood that the whites were enjoying themselves.

The white men must have looked a close-knit community to the New Guineans. There were a number of local institutions that drew the Europeans together and demonstrated the sense of community existing among the whites. Among the most important were the

sports clubs. Regular inter-town sporting contests followed by parties
and dances were a special feature of European social life in the
Morobe District during the 1930s. At the first of these, in October
1930, the Lae sports club flew to Salamaua for a weekend of snooker,
tennis and cricket, and a banquet at the hotel on the Saturday
evening. A month later the Salamaua sports club returned the visit,
and the *Rabaul Times* described the way in which 'the Laenatics
entertained the Salamaniacs':

> On Saturday night Lae spread itself out to act as hosts to the visit-
> ing team and the guests were splendidly entertained. Hats off to
> Lae when they entertain! On Sunday night the Guinea Airways
> pinnace brought the family back to Salamaua. Paddy and his friend
> tried to swim over but some thoughtless spoilsport hauled them
> aboard again none the worse for the effort.[18]

Eventually these visits became formalized, and by 1939 the Levien
trophy* was being annually awarded for the premier sporting town.
By that time five Morobe District towns—Salamaua, Lae, Wau,
Bulolo and Edie Creek—were competing in regular billiards, cricket,
tennis and athletics tournaments conducted by the Morobe Towns
Sports Association. The annual horse races at Wau were another
local sporting feature that drew the white community together. The
first race meeting was run on Boxing Day 1933, mainly as a joke, the
result of a bet between Guinea Airways' chief pilot, Ian Grabowsky,
and the manager of New Guinea Goldfields, Major G. A. Harrison,
who wagered that aviation may be able to transport heavy machinery
but could not carry livestock. Grabowsky accepted the challenge and
flew in three draught horses from Lae. The races were such a success
that a further meeting was held the next Easter, with twenty-one
horses flown in specially. After that the races took place annually and
were attended by Europeans from all over the district.[19] The New
Guineans did not participate in these sports and as a result probably
regarded them as tribal rituals of the white man.

A strong sense of communal identity and pride was apparent
among the European residents, despite Lae's close links with the
other goldfields towns and its subordinate status in relation to
Salamaua. As the town grew it became an attractive centre, admired
by visitors and vaunted by its white inhabitants. Their pride found
expression in the formation in 1933 of a citizens' association which

---

* The trophy commemorated the work of the goldfields pioneer Cecil Levien,
who died shortly before the first dredge went into operation at Bulolo in 1932.

took on the responsibility of keeping roads and reserves in good condition, planting trees and beautifying the town. Because of the efforts of the residents it was possible to observe as early as 1932 that 'from the air Lae now presents a very pleasing sight, with its smart line of European houses, surrounded by crotons of different hue and by neatly kept lawns'.[20] Newcomers to the town were usually impressed by its orderliness and efficient bustle. One visitor paid it the supreme tribute when he wrote that 'Lae in the morning light, from the deck of the 'Macdhui'* looked for all the world like some small Australian town. It is a town of big business and hidden somewhere is an impelling dynamic force, which keeps the wheels of activity moving'.[21] The citizens affectionately called their town 'Junkerville' and pointed with pride to the huge tonnages handled by the aircraft, the skill of the pilots and mechanics, the many daily trips made to the goldfields by each plane, and to the readiness and conviviality of the hospitality.

As the town spread and more Europeans arrived a number of stratifications developed within the white community. These were not so obvious in the early days of the town when most of the residents had been men and a strong egalitarian spirit, born of the common hardship entailed in founding a new industry in a new town, had existed between them. But as the pioneering stage passed and more women arrived, some of the earlier comradeship was lost and a sorting out of social groupings occurred. First there was a distinction between the Guinea Airways and Bulolo Gold Dredging staff and 'the rest', who were always in the minority. The most distinguished members of 'the rest' were the managers of Burns Philp and Vacuum Oil and the Assistant District Officer. Among the staff of the aviation and mining companies the managers and pilots considered themselves to be a class above the mechanics, clerks, storemen and 'the rest'. An early resident of Lae recalls that 'the pilots were high and mighty, highly superior creatures' who would not allow their wives to dance with any of the mechanics at any of the social events in the town. The emerging stratification into classes could be seen in the siting of the houses: 'the more pretentious residences' of the Assistant District Officer, the manager of Burns Philp and several of the pilots were built on the terrace above the airstrip, socially and geographically elevated, whereas everyone else lived on the forshore flats.[22]

---

* The *Macdhui* was a well known trading and passenger vessel operated by the trading firm Burns Philp during the 1930s. It was sunk in the Port Moresby harbour by a Japanese bomb during an air raid in 1942.

Occasionally items about the youthful town reached the international press. Usually these concerned some bizarre incident involving aircraft. On one occasion, for example, a pilot—Les Ross—crashed his plane into the upper branches of a tall tree near the end of the airstrip. Unperturbed, he simply climbed down a vine to the ground and walked back into Lae, almost casually, to find help in getting his plane down. In 1932 another pilot, Frank Drayton, crashed and died while stunt flying over the Wau airstrip. His body was brought back to Lae and buried beneath a tall mango tree on the foreshore at the end of the runway. He left behind a young wife and an infant son, who had been the first European child born in the town. Then in 1941 the town's 'first citizen', the Guinea Airways manager, Eric Chater, was killed in front of the hangars. His dog had run in front of an incoming plane, and in trying to shoo the animal out of the way he walked into the propellor. A death that momentarily focused world attention on Lae was that of the American aviatrix, Amelia Earhart Putnam, who vanished with her navigator, Captain Manning, after leaving Lae in June 1937 on the longest leg of their trip around the world. Old Lae residents still recall entertaining the couple in the Hotel Cecil the night before their departure, and then seeing them off the next morning. Their plane was so overloaded with its eight tons of fuel that it was still barely clearing the waves as it disappeared from sight, flying east along the Huon Gulf coast on its way towards Howland Island 2600 miles to the north. On such occasions Laeites, regardless of class or social position, felt they were part of history.

The New Guinean and Chinese communities

Away from work there was little contact, formal or informal, between the three communities, European, Chinese and New Guinean, and each group kept to itself. The society of the town was stratified into a strict caste system with the Europeans occupying the upper level, the New Guineans the lower, and the Chinese an uncertain position between them. The main contact between the groups was on the job, where the class structure was implicit and was rigidly maintained. Any dealings between the races proceeded on assumptions of white superiority.

The New Guineans were the town's working class. The development of Lae demanded a large body of unskilled labourers far in

excess of that available in the local villages. The labourers from outside were therefore a social element distinct from the Europeans, the
Chinese and the local villagers. How many of them were brought
into Lae is difficult to determine because they were all temporary
residents and no one kept records of their numbers. They were a
diverse group, drawn from all districts in New Guinea. More than
half of them were probably from the Morobe District, about a third
were from the Sepik, about a tenth were from Madang, with smaller
numbers from other districts. Most were employed as police, domestic servants, washermen, cleaners, carriers, stevedores, builders'
labourers, grass cutters, or general rouseabouts. They usually came to
their employers under indenture for a three-year term, and for the
most part were young single men or men without their wives. Their
numbers fluctuated according to the type of development project
being undertaken at any one time and when major works were
under way their numbers were swelled with new recruits. The
indentured workforce was also supplemented periodically by day
labour from surrounding villages, usually when a ship had arrived
with cargo to be lightered ashore. Most employers, however, preferred to have contract labourers from beyond Lae, because they
believed these were more reliable and better disciplined than the
local villagers, who had too many home connections for satisfactory
permanent employment.

The labourers were an inconspicuous group, and few visitors had
time to notice them. They lived in barracks and compounds located
at various points around the town—behind the Guinea Airways
mess, at the foot of Lo'wamung, on the western side of the aerodrome
—or in servants' quarters behind the houses of the Europeans. Their
life at work was hard and they worked long hours. Away from work
they led a dull existence, enlivened only by weekend soccer matches
on the native sports ground beside the Hotel Cecil, by interminable
games of 'lucky', a card game similar to poker, and by jaunts across
the Bumbu to visit the girls of Butibam. The labourers were an
essential group which most expatriates took for granted. Their low
wages supported the fifteen or so trade stores around the town, and
their manual labour was indispensable to most of the town's activities. Because it was assumed that at the end of their contracts they
would all depart for home, few of them established a permanent
niche for themselves in Lae society; perhaps the only ones who did
were the handful who married local village women and stayed on in
the area when their contracts had expired. The New Guinean

labourers therefore remained the invisible men of Lae, an anonymous entity forming a shadowy background to the dealings of the European and Chinese communities.

More is known about the Chinese. They began arriving in the early 1930s, usually as tradesmen working on company or government projects. Their wage rates were about half those of Europeans and many of them therefore felt the need, and saw the opportunity to run trade stores as a sideline. Some of their businesses began as off-shoots of family enterprises in Rabaul, Salamaua or Wau. As more Chinese arrived a substantial Chinatown developed on the flats between Lo'wamung and the Bumbu, north of the present Markham-Busu road. Many were married and while the men worked in town the wives and children ran the stores. Those interested in educating their children had to leave them in Rabaul, where there was a Chinese school, or send them to Hong Kong. They were an industrious group and worked hard to make a success of their stores: business started at 6 a.m. daily and a monthly turnover of £90 was considered good. Most of them eventually prospered because they practised the traditional Chinese virtues of caution, hard work and thrift. They lived quietly and their social life was restricted to occasional visits to the houses of friends for a yarn over a bottle of beer or a game of mah jong with glasses of beer as stakes.

Like the New Guinean labourers, the Chinese were a diverse group. About half of them were Cantonese, (in the main Sze Yap- and Hakka-speaking) and there were also several from Hainan, but despite these varied origins they formed a cohesive, close-knit group. They were bound by a common language, Cantonese, and the legal and unofficial discrimination they suffered at the hands of the white community. They were debarred by law from owning plantations or firearms, and from engaging in mining. They could only obtain land on short- rather than long-term leases, and they were not allowed to live or own land in the European sections of the town. Several of them managed to get around the latter obstacle by securing blocks in the European areas through European nominees. Unofficially at least they were not allowed to mix with European women or to receive treatment in the European section of the hospital, and in an earlier era of Morobe District history, they had been blamed for the worst abuses of the labour trade. They suffered these various forms of prejudice stoically and were not embittered by it. Perhaps the strongest bond linking the Chinese was the Chinese 'bank', an institution found in most towns where an expatriate Chinese com-

munity exists. The 'bank' is best described as a savings club and
emergency fund. One man acted as banker and collected a £10
monthly subscription from each member. There was thus an
accumulating kitty which could be bid for monthly by any member
wanting money urgently. To obtain the kitty or part of it a member
had to bid by offering competitive interest rates, the more urgent his
need the higher his bid. The member offering the highest bid
received the kitty and he later repaid the amount due plus interest.
Members of the 'bank' remained close to each other to safeguard their
investment, and so the 'bank' served to draw the Chinese community
together.

Lae becomes the capital of New Guinea

The administration was a late entrant into the development of Lae.
The early imperative for the build-up at Lae came entirely from the
aviation companies, and for nearly a decade the government discouraged the expansion of the town in favour of building up
Salamaua. However, an event occurred in 1937 which suddenly
altered administration prejudice against Lae. This was the disastrous
volcanic upheaval that shook Rabaul in May 1937. The eruptions
began on 29 May and continued till 3 June, depositing ash and mud
all over the town, blocking the roads and harbour, crushing trees and
houses. The entire population of 8000 New Guineans, 1000 Asians
and 800 Europeans was evacuated by boat to Kokopo twenty miles
away and could not return till 10 June. At least 427 New Guineans, 2
Europeans and 1 Chinese perished. As a result of this catastrophe the
Commonwealth government called in two vulcanologists who reported that Rabaul was likely to remain a centre of violent seismic
activity and that the early transfer of the the administrative headquarters should therefore be undertaken.[23] The Australian government accepted this advice and called on a committee headed by
Brigadier-General Tom Griffiths, a former Administrator, to tour the
Territory, inspect all possible sites and to recommend the best of
these as the place where the new capital should be built.

Griffiths presented his report in April 1938. He chose Lae and
stated in fine detail the factors influencing this decision: the climate
(which strangely enough he thought was 'healthy'), the reliable
rainfall, the absence of serious seismic activity, the central location in
relation to other districts, the absence of a large native population in
the immediate vicinity of the town that would have to be dispos-

Kamdring Bukaua, leader of the Apo group in Butibam and a prominent spokesman on village affairs

Muttu Gware, president of the Butibam Progress Association and a leader of the Ahi Association

Stephen Ahi, patron of the Ahi Association

The central commercial and administrative area of Lae, 1973

Part of the Huonville Housing Commission estate

Part of the Bumbu squatter settlement on the old village site at Buko

sessed of its land, the suitable topography and good water supply, the availability in the locality of a plentiful supply of materials for construction and of sources of power, the absence of extensive existing developments which may involve costly resumption, and the existence of well established aviation facilities. Against these merits the committee weighed certain disadvantages, the main ones being the unsuitability of Lae as a port and the high cost of transfer, which was estimated at £443 000. The committee suggested that the difficulty of a port could be overcome by placing this at Salamaua and then building a connecting road to the main centre at Lae.[24] The minister for territories, W. M. Hughes, who in his days as prime minister had been responsible for New Guinea coming under Australia's mandate, rejected these proposals summarily, and cabinet concurred. On 23 June Hughes made a long official statement to the effect that he disapproved of the Griffiths plan and had therefore chosen Salamaua as both port and capital instead. In addition he announced that a road would be built from Salamaua to Wau to link the goldfields and the coast[25]—something the goldfields community had been seeking for years.

Hughes' decision immediately sparked off a protracted and bitter debate over the rival merits of Lae and Salamaua. Hughes received great personal criticism for his apparently capricious and arbitrary action in dismissing the Griffiths report and it was hinted in the local and Australian press that Salamaua and Wau interests, in particular Burns Philp and New Guinea Goldfields, had bribed him.[26] The Australian government was accused of apathy, ignorance and irresponsibility in its attitude to New Guinea affairs. This charge was also levelled at the Territory administration, which was accused of being weak and vacillating too. In the months that followed the local and Australian press, led by the *Pacific Islands Monthly* and the *Rabaul Times*, expressed angry anti-Hughes and anti-government views. The debate widened as advocates of other capital sites advertized their claims. The New Guinea Mining Association of Wau, while applauding Hughes's promise of a road to the coast, asserted that Wau should be the capital. The businessmen of Rabaul, worried that the removal of the capital would cause a decline in trade and property value, rationalized their fears by deploring the unnecessary waste of public funds on the grounds that the eruptions were a freak occurrence unlikely to be repeated. Then a member of the Commonwealth parliament, F. Fairbairn, after a hurried tour of the Territory suggested that the separate territories of Papua and New Guinea should be combined and administered from Port Moresby. But Hughes remained impervious to all criticisms and suggestions. With exasperating wit he confirmed his opinion that Salamaua must become the capital because 'the government had a duty to prevent Rabaul becoming a second Pompeii', then went on to say that 'Adam and Eve had to be chased from the Garden of Eden by an angel with a flaming sword. We must do the same to the residents of Rabaul. Anyway Salamaua is a port and Lae is not'.[27]

The controversy had become more complicated in July 1938 when the Administrator, W. R. McNicoll, went to Salamaua with senior officials of his Public Works and Lands Department to examine the new site more closely. McNicoll, who had earlier advocated this location, now realized that the choice was the wrong one because of the high cost necessary to reclaim Salamaua's extensive swamps in order to provide sufficient land for the administration headquarters. He advised Hughes that Lae rather than Salamaua should now be the site, although he recognized that a volte face would be embarrassing to Hughes and the cabinet. Mainly because of McNicoll's change of heart federal cabinet announced through its new Minister for Territories, E. J. Harrison, that Salamaua would become a temporary capital only, pending an enquiry into the possibility of combining the administrations of Papua and New Guinea. Shortly after this he stated his intention of convening a committee to examine the question of unification and to recommend a joint capital. By this time the public of both New Guinea and Australia were becoming increasingly cynical. The Territory attitude was summed up by Gordon Thomas, the editor of the *Rabaul Times*: 'Nominations for the capital site are increasing. Once again we reiterate our suggestion that the capital remain where it has always been—Canberra.'[28] And the Canberra press corps, which had been faithfully reporting new developments for six months, caught the public mood in Australia at their annual dinner in December 1938, when they produced a satirical newspaper, *Hangover* containing a parody of the controversy under the title 'Lae off Salamaua: Capital crisis causes crater cabinet confusion':

A new crisis has arisen overshadowing the budget, the coal strike, and Hitler. Alarming tensions were created when the Prime Minister received the following urgent message from Mr. Hairbrain, M.H.R.: 'Lae off Salamaua, Joe! Natives hostile!' Mr. Hairbrain's message has created the profoundest sensation in Federal political circles. It is feared that the natives may try to make capital out of

it. The situation is fraught with grave possibilities and impossi-
bilities. Mr. Lyons summoned cabinet immediately. 'Wow!' said
the Prime Minister as he staggered from the cabinet room after the
tenth day with the problem apparently no nearer solution. 'That's
it!' yelled a chorus of weary ministers. 'Why the hell didn't we
think of Wau before?' Mr. Hughes collapsed. The crisis had
passed.[29]

The *Rabaul Times* reprinted this with great relish to allow Territory
residents to enjoy the joke on their own insularity; but the article also
underlined the insignificant part New Guinea problems played in
the minds of many Australians.

The committee called together by E. J. Harrison was chaired by
F. W. Eggleston. The report it produced, in August 1939, advised
against a combined administration for the two territories, but went
on to recommend Lae as the most desirable site for the capital of
New Guinea, for virtually the same reasons as those given by the
Griffiths committee sixteen months previously. The one difference
with the earlier report was that it discounted the lack of a harbour at
Lae and pointed out that Lae had been used successfully as a terminal for passengers, mail and heavy cargo for years; moreover Lae
and Salamaua handled the same volume of cargo at similar cost. The
committee also stressed the strategic position of Lae as the natural
outlet for the Ramu-Markham valley and the new highlands region,
where future economic development was likely to take place. In
addition it estimated the cost of the transfer to be only about
£280 000.[30] However, little was done to implement these recommendations. By the time the Australian government considered the
report, 'the war had begun and it seemed to be the wrong time to
move the administrative centre. The Australian government announced there would be no move from Rabaul for the present'.[31]
The government was also influenced by the opinion of the vulcan-
ologist in Rabaul, who believed that 'there was no danger to life in
Rabaul'.[32]

Renewed seismic activity in Rabaul soon upset this decision, however. In January 1941 severe earth tremors struck the town, followed
by landslides. Sporadic disturbances followed until 6 June, when the
Tavurvur cone again became active, spewing dust and fumes over
the town for the next three months. The bad effect on morale and
resultant decline in the efficiency of the public service led McNicoll to
advise the minister for territories (then A. M. McDonald) to effect
the transfer to Lae immediately. Canberra, in the throes of a change

of government, was apparently too preoccupied to do anything more decisive than to agree in principle. McNicoll, dissatisfied with Canberra's lack of resolution, now took the initiative. He issued a brief statement in Rabaul that the administration had decided to follow the recommendations of the Griffiths committee, and would move to Lae forthwith. Cabinet then gave belated approval, which was announced on 6 September.[33]

The transfer to Lae began in October 1941 and continued right up to the Japanese invasion in late January 1942. McNicoll himself quit Rabaul quietly on 17 November, leaving the government secretary, H. H. Page, as Deputy Administrator. He received some criticism for being among the first to leave, but he and the Executive Council had decided that the presence of the Administrator in Lae was an urgent need, to give high level direction and bring swift order out of the confused situation there. Two of the main problems he had to overcome were the opposition of the Rabaul business community, who resisted the move because they stood to lose financially, and the apathy and inertia of his own staff. Neither group supported him and each was nettled by the suddenness of his decision and the confusion it produced. But in view of the apparent danger of imminent volcanic upheaval and the lack of support and direction from Canberra, McNicoll can hardly be condemned.[34] The Administrator arrived unobtrusively in the new capital. He slipped into Lae aboard his yacht on Sunday afternoon 23 November and made his official landing the next morning at nine o'clock. The *Rabaul Times*, ever an organ preaching white superiority, had hoped for an ostentatious ceremony in Lae 'to signal the fact that this one-time headquarters of an aviation company has now become the capital of the Territory' because 'pomp and ceremony impresses the native mind, and is about the only white characteristic that really does impress our native population'.[35] But the only ones waiting to greet the Administrator and thus to witness Lae's final rise to capital status after many years of wrangling were 'the police guard, administration officials and about 30-odd of the general public'.[36]

Today the most surprising element in the four years of complicated manoeuvring preceding the transfer to Lae is the total lack of participation by the New Guinean community, few of whom would have known what was afoot. The sole references to New Guineans in all the discussions over the choice of a capital site were the brief observations of the Griffiths and Eggleston committees that Lae was suitable because of 'the absence of a large native population that would have to be dispossessed of its land'.[37] The Eggleston committee had actually wondered if it should obtain the evidence of New Guineans, but was assured that 'on a subject of this kind native opinion did not exist'.[38] Pre-war New Guinea clearly operated on colonial assumptions: the governors and the governed dwelt in separate circles which intersected but rarely and then on terms dic-tated by the former. In the search for the capital site the New Guineans remained mute. The controversy was not of their making, nor did it generally affect them. It was part of Australian history and therefore considered to be none of their business.

War in the Pacific

The new glory of Lae proved ephemeral, so that the bustle and activity that took place after the transfer was in vain. McNicoll launched into a hurried public works programme to provide the new capital with essential offices and residences. The residents were re-ported to be 'anticipating their town becoming one of the most modern capitals in the southern hemisphere', although they recog-nized 'that the transition will take time'.[39] By the end of November 1941 a Lands Office, Crown Law Office, Central Administration building, Post Office, Treasury, storage sheds and Government House were all nearing completion; work had begun on a Salamaua–Lae–Wau–Bulolo telephone link; and consideration was being given to post-war development according to a plan drawn up in 1938. Much confusion arose from the fact that the Administrator and some departments were in Lae, others temporarily in Salamaua, and still others with the Deputy Administrator in Rabaul. Nor did jockeying for advantage among the citizens and public servants help. McNicoll had to deal with many requests like that of the man who wanted to know 'Will there be a Government Printer? When will a European school be started? When will a medical officer be stationed here? etc. etc. etc.'[40] Other problems were the lack of adequate shopping facili-ties, the extortionate charges of the only store, Burns Philp, the inefficiency of the mail system, and the slow progress of the house building programme. McNicoll battled valiantly to overcome all of these, but to little avail, for he had only been in Lae a fortnight when the Pacific War began with the Japanese attack on Pearl Harbor on 7 December 1941.

McNicoll soon received orders for the evacuation of all women and children and this took place in a hurried airlift from Lae to Port Moresby. Rabaul was bombed on 4 January 1942 and it was obvious that the Morobe towns would soon receive similar treatment. He was busy making arrangements for the evacuation of Rabaul and preparing for his administration to fall back on Wau when the Japanese struck. They attacked Lae, Salamaua and Bulolo shortly after noon on 21 January, swooping in low to machine-gun and bomb the three places. In Lae there had been some warning, as a radio message had been received from a coast-watcher at Finschhafen saying that about sixty planes were on their way. Guinea Airways had time to fly out some of the planes at Lae before the Japanese could bomb the town. The attack lasted forty-five minutes and either flattened or severely damaged nearly every building. There were few casualties, however, because the residents had taken shelter in slit trenches which they had dug previously. After the attack they salvaged what they could, then destroyed the fuel stocks, motor cars and remaining documents before abandoning the town. There were complaints that 'natives, Chinese and one or two Europeans broke into the Burns Philp store and looted the liquor supplies. Large numbers of natives got drunk'.[41] Some Europeans were able to fly out, but most had to undergo a tough eight days' walk through the rain to Wau. The local people temporarily abandoned their villages to retreat into the bush. The indentured labourers had similarly gone into hiding or had started to walk home, some going as far as the Sepik. Those Chinese who had not walked to Wau moved out of town to shelter with the villagers.

McNicoll had been seriously ill with malaria and pneumonia and could not be evacuated. By night he slept in Jacobsen's house and by day he was carried down to the swamp behind the present Bugandi High School to shelter in a rough hut. He handed over the administration to the senior military officer at Lae, Major E. W. Jenyns, on 21 January, and on 24 January he was able to fly to Wau, and then to Port Moresby and on to Australia. In the meantime a company of the New Guinea Volunteer Rifles, containing a number of Lae residents, remained behind in the area around Jacobsen's poultry farm. The Japanese finally landed at 4.45 a.m. on 8 February. Lae's three month period as the capital of New Guinea thus ended as it had begun, in confusion.

6

THE TOWN, THE MISSIONARIES AND THE PEOPLE

For all the brisk activity of its aviation industry, Lae in the 1930s was never much more than a minor town in the tropics. Incongruously built in a clearing that had been carved out of the jungle at the water's edge, it was a town that rarely rated attention anywhere else but in the parochial columns of the *Rabaul Times*. But despite its relative lack of importance in the world scale of events, its development was enormously significant for the people living in the villages on its fringes. As it grew it effected far-reaching changes on their society because it made heavy demands on them. The mission, too, which had earlier been one of the main agents of change, continued to make heavy demands on their time and energy. The townspeople and the missionaries were often at odds, however, and were frequently in competition for the loyalty of the people. In the face of the conflicting requirements of town and mission, the people had to reassess their attitude towards both, and so the 1930s was a disturbing period of readjustment for the Lae villagers.

The influence of the town

Colonial towns were often built with the sweat of vast armies of native labourers. Lae was no excepion, despite the high level of mechanization in its aviation industry, for it depended on the physical exertions of innumerable New Guineans. Much of the work —unloading barges, stacking oil drums, carrying cargo—was not of a regular nature, and as a result many men from local villages were employed on a casual day to day basis whenever some urgent job had to be done. This happened so frequently that many local men worked in Lae almost full time and were involuntarily drawn into the life of the town as a result. Although heavy demands on village labour preceded the foundation of the town, the need for labourers exceeded all previous demands on the villages once the town was established. The sources of labour were now exploited to the limit to satisfy the needs of the aviation industry and of the goldfields generally. A contemporary government report described the 'abnormal' situation as the gold rush mounted during 1926–7:

> The influx of so many miners feverishly eager to work their claims was responsible for an ever increasing demand for native labour, to obtain which almost fantastic figures began to be offered. The Morobe District was handiest and was combed for native labourers. These became daily more sought after and yet more difficult to obtain. The very arduous nature of cargo carrying and the numerous deaths from dysentery etc. that occurred among natives intensified the disinclination of many of the Morobe natives to recruit willingly.[1]

This report estimated the number of labourers employed on the goldfields at the height of the rush at 3200, or about a quarter of the entire contract labour force in the Territory. Before the rush the Morobe District had not been an important source of labour in comparison to other districts: previously men from the Morobe District had always been less than 5 per cent of the Territory contract labour force. But by 1928 the district was providing 17 per cent of all new recruits and Morobe men by then amounted to 13 per cent of all contract labourers.[2]

The severity of the labourer's conditions and their reaction against this were reflected in the extremely high death and desertion rates on the goldfields. Before the rush Morobe men had figured insignificantly in the annual deaths of labourers under contract: they were generally less than 3 per cent of the total. But during the early development of the goldfields the mortality rate soared, and their deaths amounted to more than 23 per cent of all deaths in the workforce. Similarly, in former times desertions by Morobe men had always been less than 10 per cent of the total number of desertions for the Territory, but during the rush their desertions reached 34 per cent of the annual total. The demand for Morobe labourers continued to be high until the war: after 1933–4 Morobe men were never less than 30 per cent of the entire Territory contract labour force, and after 1932–3 the Morobe District always supplied more than 26 per cent of the new recruits.[3]

Because of their proximity to the goldfields port of Salamaua the Lae were inevitably drawn into the labour trade in large numbers.

In one of his reports Schmutterer described how 'nearly every week the people are forced to carry the packs of the whites. Dysentery has claimed many victims. If this slavery is not soon ended the most evil consequences will befall the people and the mission'.[4] News of the appalling conditions on the goldfields filtered back to the coastal villages. One Lae man who was at Edie Creek wrote a letter home warning his friends not to come up to the goldfields because one of his friends who was ill had stopped beside the track to rest on the walk in and had not been seen again. This disturbed a number of the men so much that they fled to Malahang plantation, where they pretended to be mission labourers, to escape being press-ganged into service on the goldfields.

As demands for labour became more clamorous and the district scoured more thoroughly by the recruiters, the possibility of illegal recruiting increased proportionately. It was not long before the missionaries were once again making vociferous complaints to Rabaul about recruiting malpractices. They asserted that government officials and recruiters were operating together and using teams of armed natives to engage recruits forcibly in many parts of the Huon Peninsula and the Markham valley. 'For the sake of the goldfields hundreds of natives are being sacrificed', they claimed in a submission to the League of Nations.[5] Even from Rabaul it was obvious that Morobe District recruiting had once more become a scandal. The administration could no longer afford to turn a blind eye to the situation as it had often done during the period of military rule. Under pressure from the Permanent Mandates Commission and the International Labour Organization, who were advising that 'the only remedy lay in a rigorous supervision of the methods of recruiting',[6] the administration in late 1927 appointed a committee under Judge B. Montagu Phillips to enquire into the allegations of the Missionaries. As the committee went about its task a nasty tale of co-operation between the government officials and recruiters in impressing, beating, intimidating and molesting village people emerged. It became clear that most Europeans involved had committed serious breaches of the labour ordinance, and some had been guilty of the most depraved behaviour. The central figure in the investigations was a warrant officer of police, Christopher Hawkes, who had the job of obtaining recruits for the government. Phillips found that Hawkes was an overbearing, vicious bully who was not fit to be entrusted with the task of supervising recruiting because of his great contempt for New Guineans. In a number of villages he had assembled the village people and demanded recruits. If he could not get the number he wanted he beat up the *luluais* and *tultuls* before the assembled people, then selected the men he wanted. Hawkes was subsequently dismissed from the service, brought to trial, convicted and sentenced to eighteen months' gaol.[7] The suspicion remains, however, that he was but a scapegoat chosen to save face for a lax administration.

After this the worst abuses of the trade were eliminated, but labour conditions in the Morobe District continued to cause the Mandates Commission grave concern throughout the 1930s. The commission was particularly worried by the unwillingness of the recruits and the coercion needed to obtain them, by the high mortality and desertion rates among the labourers, and by the over-recruitment of the men in some of the villages. In particular it pointed to the fact that at most times almost a third of the enumerated adult males in New Guinea were under contract.[8] The various Australian delegates sent to the League of Nations responded evasively to the questions and criticisms of the commission. The commission acted from humanitarian motives, but its pleas fell on the ears of a government that appeared unwilling to take heed, for the conditions the commission wished to ameliorate persisted throughout the rule of the pre-war civil administration. As one scholar has observed, 'the administration was almost driven to choose between allowing abuses in recruiting and checking the rate of economic development. In one respect—that of countenancing an extremely heavy drain on manpower from the native areas—Australia unhesitatingly adopted the former course'.[9]

Although recruitment levels remained high in the Morobe District throughout the pre-war period, the actual demand for plantation and goldfield labourers from the immediate Lae area slackened considerably after 1930. There were three reasons for this: the decline in copra production following the world depression of 1929 caused a lessening in demand for plantation labourers, and the depressed plantations could not compete with the healthy mining industry for the available labour; the introduction of the aviation service obviated the need for a vast workforce of carriers to keep open the supply lines; and finally, as Lae developed as the hub of the aviation system, it became a magnet for all available local labour.[10] But although the Lae were not needed so much for plantation and mining work, the demand on their services remained high, because the development of the town merely meant a shift in the type of labour they were required to perform. Instead of carrying cargo between Salamaua and

Wau or operating the sluices at Edie Creek as contract labourers, they now had to work as casual day-labourers in the burgeoning town across the Bumbu.

The village men did not have the option of withholding their services, despite government claims that compulsory labour did not exist in the Territory. Indirect coercion by the means of the head tax forced the men out to work as wage labourers as soon as they left school. For the European employers in the town the villagers counted mainly as units of labour. That they had a separate, complex and valid life away from the job does not seem to have occurred to any-one but the missionaries, one of whom complained that 'the Masters believe the people have nohing to do. Almost every day the men go off to carry cargo in the town. Sundays are not observed and the natives are not allowed to take exception'.[11] As the needs of the town became more urgent during the 1930s, so its labour requirements increased and the local villages were inevitably affected. It became a frequent complaint of the missionaries that the men were so over-worked they were not attending daily devotions in the villages, they were too tired to spend any time in the club houses, and they had little time to attend to such essential matters as maintaining their houses and gardens.[12] They were being forced out of their customary occupation as subsistence gardeners and away from their role as the upholders of village traditions and skills, and were becoming mere unskilled urban wage-labourers instead. Under these circumstances the drastic alteration of the social fabric of the Lae villages was unavoidable.

Just as disruptive as the heavy demands made on village men to work as labourers was the arrival of hundreds of migrants, European, New Guinean and Chinese. As most of the migrants were single men, they sought out the local women and introduced a new element into the village social system—prostitution. During the 1930s the missionaries frequently had to complain that

> many of the young girls have lost their earlier shyness and are hanging around the town and the contract workers are night and day in the villages. Their search for clothes, jewellery and rice, and the opportunity to procure these from the town boys have built many questionable connections. Particularly in Butibam the moral laxity that is prevalent gives us plenty of reason to be worried.[13]

The village women acquired the reputation of being promiscuous as they catered for the needs of the town. One early resident recalls that 'prostitutes from the local villages played an important part round the mid-1930s and a bit before'.[14] One of them was 'owned' collectively by several of the pilots and it was not unknown for the police to arrest the girls and keep them overnight for interrogation. The result of such developments was a great upheaval in the rigid traditional morality. The state of flux could be seen in the behaviour of the elders and evangelists, the exemplars of Lutheran virtue. By 1938 the missionary was lamenting the fact that so many of them had been guilty of 'continuous moral transgression' he had few elders left who had not been excluded from the congregation.[15]

Another new element was marriage between village women and the migrant men. Traditionally marriages had been arranged only with neighbouring villages, but now the people began marrying beyond these limits. The village elders were concerned by 'foreign' marriages because they feared that these would dilute the village blood and weaken their hold over the land, which they did not wish to share with outsiders. At first they endeavoured to force the outsiders who had married local girls to live in separate settlements beyond the villages to minimize their influence and discourage other girls from marrying outside. But these measures proved ineffectual, for the contract labourers had wealth enough to entice the girls into marriage and to encourage their parents to release them.[16] Traditional social controls were breaking down in any case and as a result the elders were unable to prevent headstrong young girls from marrying outside. New marriage patterns were being formed and whatever action the elders took was probably in vain: the trend towards outside marriage has continued to the present day, and nowadays up to 70 per cent of marriages in the Lae villages take place with outside partners.[17]

The question of marriage led the people into a bitter dispute with the missionaries. It arose because of the moral frailty of the evangelists, many of whom had to work away from home and as a result were not subject to the same degree of moral restraint as people in the home villages. They were often lonely men because they felt superior to the members of their flocks and remained aloof, believing they had to maintain the superior status of the coastal culture of which they were the bearers. Many of them found release in sexual encounters with women of the flock whose husbands were away on labour services. People in the inland villages were suspicious of single evangelists and sometimes warned the missionary, 'If you do not get your evangelist married soon, we will send him back to you'.[18]

Because of the number of evangelists who fell, the missionaries realized that all mission workers on outstations should be married. They therefore attempted to force their evangelists to marry; and the home villages had to supply the brides. Mission interference in the village marriage system was not welcomed. A family offering a girl in marriage to an evangelist might not get what it regarded as a fair economic return for her, for the evangelist lived outside the village and brought little wealth into it; moreover he was not available for many co-operative tasks. Families preferred their girls to marry wealthy men living in the home village—returned contract labourers, for example—because these men could offer gifts and help in group tasks. Parents were therefore reluctant to release their daughters to the mission; as a result they came into serious conflict with the missionaries, who could not appreciate the fact that the gift exchanges and reciprocal obligations of marriage were an important part of the traditional economic system and could not easily be tampered with. One of the missionaries, Hans Maurer (who succeeded Schmutterer in 1935), was so incensed at the people's refusal to co-operate in the marriage arrangements he wished to make that he punished them by withholding Holy Communion and baptism from the congregation.[19] The missionaries' attitude to marriage also tended to alienate the evangelists. Only the less attractive girls—those with physical defects, the ones least likely to obtain a good bride price—were offered voluntarily to an evangelist, who thus had reason to resent his spouse, his vocation and the mission. He was therefore likely to neglect his bride and this only compounded the growing hostility of the people.[20] When the missionary acted as marriage broker he thus upset many people and aroused their resentment against the mission. This served to reduce its authority and to weaken the influence of the congregation in village affairs.

The compelling influence of the town was most obvious amongst the younger villagers. The town weaned the young people away from their elders, deepening the earlier rift that had been caused by education and literacy, and in this way helped undermine the traditional forms of social control within the villages. It offered the young people attractive alternatives to the social, religious and economic order their elders wished to uphold. Working for the townspeople gave them freedom from traditional restraints and obligations and allowed them to share in the consumer society of the West through the possessions of their employers. The young people generally shared the attitude of a Kamkumung youth who told one of the missionaries that 'in the town it is beautiful to be free, without ties and without worries. Why should we work in the sun planting taro? With the Misis or Master cooking and washing is not hard work. One hardly needs to sweat. Also they never threaten us with the Gospel and they allow us to do some things which are not permitted in the village'.[21] The villages could not match such allurements. As the town drew the young people away from the customary ways of the village, where group membership, familial duty and obligation to one's neighbours had been the basis of all personal relationships, it also effected a change in the villager's attitude towards himself and others. In Lae he found he was an individual, a separate being who could live by and for himself. This was not so in the village and Schmutterer, who knew the village society well and valued its co-operative basis, saw how the town was inevitably making individuals of people who had customarily been members of a group. 'The influence of the materialism of our culture is becoming stronger all the time', he sadly observed. 'It is a sneaky poison which works without fail'.[22]

With encouragement from the missionaries the elders opposed the influence the town was having on the young people. They agreed with the missionaries that the young men were picking up bad habits while they were away on labour service and they resented the fact that 'these young men have a lot of cheek and a chip on their shoulders. They are a great hindrance with their new magic and love potions, and make the people so afraid that they are virtually the masters of the village'.[23] They saw that the town was aggravating this problem further and shared the missionaries' belief that 'the youths are flippant and superficial. So much beckons to them from outside that the old customs and the village cannot compete and so one tie after another breaks'.[24] They railed against the young and lamented the failure of the traditional restraints for keeping the village youth in check: 'We take them to the government and they are put in gaol for a few days, but that is just a pleasant time for them', they complained. 'Earlier on we took out our spears and then there was peace, but today we have no power'.[25] The elders longed for the days gone by when they had dignity and respect and the village social system was based on their preeminence. However, they recognized that new times had come and that their objections were in vain for it suited the townspeople for the youths to be at work in Lae rather than in the village following tradition. 'That is the white man and his custom and there is little we can do about it', they were forced to admit.[26] There were now new systems of social control—the European employer, the labour gang, the *kiap's* court—which were dislodging the customary system. The old men had to resign themselves to the fact that the young people were no longer prepared to accept the tyranny of traditions ordained by their elders, and that village custom was disintegrating as a result.

The disintegration was obvious in a number of directions. One example was the gradual abandonment of morning and evening devotions, which had long been held in each village under the leadership of the elders. The elders now found that the youths were refusing to attend and when chided simply laughed the matter off, pointing out that 'the whites go without prayers and sermons and are better off than the missionaries'.[27] Rather than take the ridicule of the young, some elders simply stopped calling their villages to devotions. The irreligiousness of the white community was also an important influence, for some of the Europeans actively opposed the work of the mission by deriding those villagers who professed Christianity and telling them their faith was founded on a lie. This weakened the force of traditional authority as it persuaded the young people to reject what the congregational leaders and missionaries ordained. The missionaries, like the elders, deprecated the decay of the old order, ironically without realizing that they were the spearhead of the very 'penetration of the culture of the whites' they deplored.[28] Their sympathies lay all with the elders, who were bemused by the steady decline of their authority, the loss of the old customs, the release of the young, and the changing social order. The missionaries were conservatives, and in a situation where the social order was changing rapidly they were as much out of touch with the course of events as were the elders.

As the village connections weakened and many of the younger villagers became assimilated into the town community, new patterns of living emerged. Some worked as domestic servants, which entailed residence in the town rather than in the village, and some who lived in the village worked in the town full-time. This meant reduced contact with the village because town workers did not have much time for the tasks and duties of the village: gardening, house building, patronage of the men's club, and observation of the religious duties required by congregational membership. The workers participated in the cash economy and urban society of the town rather than in the subsistence agriculture and traditional society of the village; they were thus becoming townsmen. And the village, instead of serving its traditional functions, was becoming a place of residence for an urban workforce.

The coming of the Chinese trade stores played an important part in the process of Westernizing the villagers and drawing them into the life of the town. The stores gave the people ready access to a wide range of European manufactured goods and foods—metal cooking utensils, knives and axes, matches, lamps, garments, mirrors, soap, paints, tea, bread, sugar, rice and tinned meat—and they tended to become dependent on these. One of the missionaries complained that 'many of the natives are wasting their money in order to buy goods in the Chinese trade stores, and although they earn much more than formerly they still have no money'.[29] Rather than simply wasting their money it is more likely that the people were demonstrating their appreciation of the cash economy. They had money and it was easier for them to buy food and goods than to produce these themselves by the old methods. They were clearly departing from the customary subsistence economy of the village and were being assimilated into the cash economy of the town. The changes in dress, diet and daily tasks that were implicit in the mounting reliance on trade store goods also pointed to a fading of the traditional material culture and a loss of customary skills. Although this process preceded the foundation of the town, it accelerated rapidly afterwards. The people were clearly moving away from what has been described as 'an economy that is . . . viable and self sufficient at the level of primitive affluence' to one that was 'almost entirely dependent on external aid, and on the importation of foreign skills and capital'.[30]

The assimilation of the villages into the town community caused consternation for the elders without greatly bothering the young people, but one of the by-products of European settlement that greatly disturbed all villagers was a series of influenza epidemics which swept through the villages after 1917. The first, in 1917, claimed eighty lives and prompted the people at Buko to move to the present Butibam site, which they thought was healthier because it was higher and better drained. Further debilitating recurrences followed almost annually after that. One of the most serious was in 1931 when a foreign ship brought the disease to both Salamaua and Lae, where 'without exception the whole population came down with it'.[31] By the time it had run its course several months later 'a third of all the children in Lae had neither father nor mother'.[32] The onslaught of the epidemics greatly perplexed the people. In 1931 they first blamed the recent *Sam* festival at Salamaua, where a num-

Houses in Butibam, 1973

The village chapel in Butibam, used for prayer meetings and meetings of the village elders

The new community centre serving the Two Mile migrant settlement

The men's meeting house, Butibam, 1973

ber of people had contracted the disease, but as the death toll mounted they turned back to the church in terror: 'We have sinned and it is the hand of God. We have to atone for our sins. So preached the evangelist Matai at every grave'.[33] The missionaries do not appear to have rejected this mediaeval interpretation, possibly because they themselves believed that the deaths were part of divine retribution. What most disturbed the people was the failure of Christianity to halt the attrition. The missionaries conducted special prayer meetings, but these produced little effect and simply showed that Christianity was not infallible. As a result some of the people tried to find an explanation in the old religion and whenever epidemics broke out they sought relief through curative magic spells; thus when prayers failed during the 1931 epidemic a group of people tried to end the disease by sacrificing a dog.

The high death rate caused by influenza did not greatly perturb the expatriate employers in the town. Possibly they thought that as New Guinea was an unhealthy place death from chronic disease was nothing unusual for New Guineans. There is no record of action by either the company medical orderlies or the government medical officers to curb the epidemics. Indeed when ships arrived to discharge cargo the people were still expected to turn up and help unload them, regardless of the number of villagers who were ill.[34] Each outbreak of influenza seemed to induce a mood of apathy and lethargy among the people; perhaps this was in part due to the depressing knowledge that for them it was work as usual in spite of their afflictions.

The difficulties of the mission

The mission continued to expand for several years after the foundation of Lae, despite the distracting influence of the town, and as late as 1932 the missionary was able to boast that 'in no year since its origin has the congregation grown so rapidly'.[35] But as the 1930s wore on a number of serious tensions developed in the relationship between the people and the mission, and in consequence of this many of the villagers deserted the church. The missionaries themselves were much to blame for the disaffection of the people. Their inflexibility in imposing their beliefs and attitudes and their lack of sympathy for anything but orthodox and fundamentalist protestant Christianity helped to destroy the confidence and pride of the people.

This eventually alienated many villagers and drove them away from the church.

Nowhere was the intolerance of the missionaries more obvious than in their attitude to the traditional religion. They had so rigorously suppressed paganism whenever they found evidence of it that within several decades they had thoroughly eradicated outward signs of the old beliefs and only an imprecise memory of magic spells remained. This could be seen in the fact that by the mid 1930s, when some people were again turning to the old faith, they had forgotten so much that they had to call in spell casters from outside.[36] However, vestiges of pagan religion continued to emerge, particularly at times of crisis. In 1934, for example, when the wife of one of the Butibam teachers fell ill with peritonitis her mother called in a Laewomba magician to cast curative spells after the combined efforts of both the mission and government doctors and the prayers of the congregation had failed to cure her. On such occasions the missionaries displayed their lack of appreciation for the deep personal anguish of the afflicted. Generally they over-reacted, taking such severe measures as refusing to celebrate Holy Communion to show their displeasure. Cases such as that of the teacher's wife were slight and amounted to no more than the use of simple curative magic, rather than a full-scale reversion to pagan religion. The missionaries nevertheless feared the latter, as even the most harmless magic showed they had failed in one of their prime aims: to root out paganism entirely. Their response on each occasion weakened their influence with the people for it taught them that basically Westerners despised their culture and had little appreciation of their deepest needs.

The reappearance of spell-casting illustrated a number of important cross-currents within the villages. On each occasion when magic became a public issue the congregation divided between those who approved of spells and those who supported the views of the missionaries. The teacher whose wife died from peritonitis, for example, was so angered when he discovered his mother-in-law had called in a magician that he reported the matter to the missionary. The mission had not completely lost the loyalty of the villagers and could still rely on a substantial bloc of support; however, some people were beginning to realize that Western religion (and science) was not omnipotent and that there were cases where it failed. While the missionaries might ascribe the failure of their prayers to inscrutable divine will, this was not a satisfying rationalization for people who desired results or were not satisfied with the results delivered by Christianity. Such people had nothing to lose by returning to traditional practices.

As World War II approached it became obvious that the pagan religion was far from dead. The missionary was forced to concede that 'the old heathenism is not dead and won't be for a long time yet'.[37] He had just had an experience in Wagang which showed that some of the old beliefs were not only surviving but were being passed on to the younger generations. One of the elders of the Wagang congregation had been injured in an accident near a place formerly hallowed because of the spirits the people believed dwelt there. He asked several schoolboys to pray for him; but instead of going into the church and praying to the Christian God as the missionary had taught them, they went to the spot where the accident occurred and prayed to the ancestral spirits. Afterwards they stated that they had actually seen a spirit. More and more incidents like this occurred and it became clear that many people were turning to the old ideas about ancestral and other spirits to explain various daily experiences. Traditional religion had explained many of the phenomena of nature by the supernatural, and many natural events were taken as omens from a whole host of spirits, both evil and benign. Whatever explanations Europeans might give for daily events—supernatural ('the will of God') or natural (climatic, biological, psychological)—these were inadequate for villagers who did not share the same conceptual background. The missionaries went to great lengths to show how the old beliefs were anti-Christian superstition and that 'it was a step back into unbelief and heathen imagination',[38] but the fact remained that Christianity could not satisfactorily explain things that puzzled the people. As a religion that is primarily concerned with the state of the individual's soul and his relationship to God and other men, it does not interpret physical events: science fulfils that role for Westerners. Traditional religion on the other hand explained the material as well as the nonmaterial world. Christianity was therefore failing the people as it did not satisfy their curiosity about the physical universe. The assurances the missionaries may have been able to give did not convince them, because these were probably as far-fetched to them as their ideas were to the missionaries. In reverting to their former beliefs they were thus asserting the value of their own culture.

The question of language was another stumbling block for the missionaries, despite the great success they had enjoyed in spreading Yabem. In the mountains of the Huon Peninsula, where most languages are Non-Austronesian, they used Kâte, a Non-Austronesian language of the Finschhafen area, rather than Yabem. Because the Lae circuit comprised both Austronesian and Non-Austronesian speakers, the mission transferred the Waing and Nabak regions to the Kâte district, as this meant a more rational use of mission resources. This was done in 1932 when the Reverend Gustav Bergmann, a Kâte missionary, opened a station at Boana. Gradually more and more of the Non-Austronesian villages of the Lae circuit were transferred to Bergmann's circuit. The decision to make this transfer greatly perturbed the Lae congregation. The Lae had developed a proprietorial attitude towards the inland peoples because they had sponsored the foundation of the inland stations and had come to regard the inland as their private mission field. They could not therefore see the rationale behind the mission's move, and interpreted this as an affront. Their pride was so sorely wounded that they vowed never again to help with mission extension. Schmutterer, who knew his Lae congregation well, had foreseen this difficulty and as early as 1925 had counselled against any interference with the circuit boundaries. He therefore resisted the encroachment of Kâte into his district and subsequently had some cutting comments to make about his young colleague in Boana, whom he accused of trespassing on Lae territory.[39] The affront to the Lae had a serious effect on the church. Mission work in the hinterland had become one of the chief reasons for the existence of the Lae congregation. The schools in the coastal villages were geared to produce mission workers for the inland, and among the highest points of achievement for a Lae man was service on one of the out-stations. Thus the mission's action in transferring parts of the Lae circuit to the Kâte district could only undermine the congregational structure.

The congregation's decision not to take part in further evangelization came at an awkward time for the mission, for it threatened to disrupt the extension of the Lutheran faith into the central highlands of New Guinea. Because of what Johann Flierl described as 'a vicious race for supremacy' between the Lutherans and the Roman Catholics in the newly explored highlands region in the mid 1930s,[40] the Lutherans were anxious to open up as many evangelists' posts as possible in the new districts around present day Kundiawa and

Mount Hagen. Well established coastal congregations were therefore pressured into supplying as many men as possible and some missionaries went to extraordinary lengths to recruit volunteers. Maurer, for example, closed the central Ampo church twice for lengthy periods and preached only in the villages, devoting all his sermons to the theme of evangelization as a means of reawakening the interest of the congregation in mission extension. Apparently his ruse worked, because each time the villages offered men despite their earlier decision not to assist. But their hearts were no longer in the work; they had lost interest and their weekly collections were barely enough to pay the mission workers from the congregation who were posted inland.[41] The people had been further insulted by the mission's decision to use Kâte in the highlands region. Once again this had been a rational decision on the part of the mission, because the highlanders all spoke Non-Austronesian languages. The people did not interpret the mission's action in such reasoned terms and believed it to be a mission stratagem for minimizing the influence of the Yabem district. The Lae were proud of their coastal culture and were ready to take offence if they thought it was being slighted. They could not become enthusiastic about work that projected the culture of a rival, especially when they thought the missionaries were deceiving them. Maurer complained that the use of Kâte in the highlands had destroyed his credibility among the people, pointing out to his superiors that 'without their confidence in me not much is possible';[42] to his dismay he realized that the mission had unwittingly given the people a reason for withdrawing from the church.

Although the reappearance of the traditional religion and the problems of language and mission extension worried the missionaries, their greatest headaches were caused by the evangelists and teachers. The moral frailty of the mission workers was but a part of the problem; equally important was their discontentment in the role to which the mission had assigned them. In earlier years they had been the elite of the Christian congregation and had enjoyed high status both within the home village and on the mission field. But as the town developed it offered seductive alternatives to labour for the mission and the missionaries found that they were unable to compete with it because they could not offer their workers the benefits available there. The problem of the mission workers is illustrated by the example of T., a teacher whom Schmutterer regarded as his most able and reliable assistant: 'his whole life had been dedicated to the

work of the mission', the missionary wrote. 'He was talented and
friendly with an outgoing personality that made him liked by whites
and blacks alike'.[43] T. became dissatisfied with his lot as a teacher
at a distant outpost because he believed he was not earning enough
to support his large family. He remained unconvinced when the
missionary assured him 'he had a good life on his station; the
people made his gardens and he had plenty of food'.[44] Schmutterer
discovered through the confession of a woman in Lae that T. had
committed adultery. In view of the fact that T. had recently treated
his sister rather shabbily after she had given birth to an illegitimate
baby, the missionary refused to greet the teacher next time he came to
Lae, because he had been offended by his hypocrisy. T. then compounded his errors by writing a letter to Schmutterer accusing him
of being unfriendly; the missionary replied, countercharging T.
with dishonesty. He now came humbly to the missionary, begging
forgiveness and seeking permission to return to his station. Schmutterer granted this request, but T. did not return to his school. He
remained in Lae instead and took a job on the wharf, where he was
killed in an accident several days later. The missionary believed his
death represented divine retribution, noting that 'he will not be
quickly forgotten in Lae for the reason that the Lord sent his
punishment down in the form of death'.[45] This was a concept the
people understood well, for the traditional religion had emphasized
it and Christianity confirmed it. One of the Labu elders underlined
this fact when he told the dying teacher, 'If you had gone back to
your school you would not have had to die,'[46] The fall of T. demonstrated a number of problems the mission was having with its
workers. Their continued sexual indiscretions were perhaps a sign
that they could not maintain the high standards required by their
role. They were disenchanted with the material rewards of their
work and they saw that their isolation on the outposts was denying
them the material wealth available to their relatives at home. As a
result they lost their sense of vocation and loyalty to the mission.
Without their enthusiastic support the mission could carry on only
under difficulty, and as their dedication evaporated much of the
mission task became a meaningless ritual performed only because it
was habitual.

As the people's support of the mission dwindled during the 1930s
it became a common lament of the missionaries that 'the coastal
people are slipping away from the path of Christianity more and

more'.[47] Much of their declining interest in Christianity can be explained by a deterioration in their bond with the missionaries. One of the main reasons for this was the increasing impersonality of the link between the missionaries and the people, in part a result of the decreasing amount of time the missionaries spent among the villagers. In the early days of the mission Schmutterer had won the loyalty of the people by dwelling among them and showing that he was their personal pastor. However, as the inland mission expanded he had to spend several months of each year patrolling the outposts, and so he, and Maurer after him, had less contact with the Lae. They delegated more and more of their personal duties—baptismal instruction, daily meditation and prayers, visiting the sick—to the elders and evangelists. This was only proper if the congregation was to become truly autonomous, but it allowed their relationship with the people to become more impersonal. Without an intimate bond forged through common experience and understanding, relations between the villagers and the missionaries tended to become more like those between the villagers and the townspeople.

The development of the mission holding at Malahang was important in contributing to this depersonalization. As we have seen, the establishment of the plantation tended to formalize the bond between the mission and the people, making an employer of the one and an employee of the other. Malahang subsequently became a centre of great activity. After the mission set up its own aviation service in 1935–6, Malahang grew much as Lae had nine years previously. The mission was developing this area to replace Finschhafen as the mission headquarters when the eruption of the war in Europe and the internment of German missionaries in Australia in 1939 prevented further work. As the centre of the mission aviation system Malahang had a constant stream of visitors and 'mission personnel were coming, staying and going all the time, not only the whites but many more New Guineans, evangelists, teachers, elders'.[48] Because there was no guest house at Malahang most visitors had to stay at Ampo and this kept the Lae missionaries busy. Even before the introduction of mission aviation the missionaries used to complain about the number of guests they had to put up, and in 1931 alone there had been 600 'guest days'. Consequently, bothered with guests, the missionaries were deprived of contact with the people and their pastoral work suffered as a result.

The missionaries' dealings with the townspeople also affected their connection with the villagers. They generally enjoyed cordial relations with the Europeans of the town and formed friendships with a number of them. Some of the townspeople made a habit of walking across to Ampo to pay a social call of a Sunday afternoon and they looked on Ampo as a 'place where one meets with great hospitality'.[49] In return the missionaries believed 'it would be ridiculous to withdraw from them because of some of their unpleasant elements' and Schmutterer regretted the fact 'that my English is not better so that I cannot give them more intellectually'.[50] Having created amicable links with the town, the missionaries were more prepared to compromise with the townspeople on some important issues. Although they opposed the abuses of the labour trade, they adopted a conciliatory approach towards the town's demands for village labour; thus one of them was able to write, 'It would be wrong to be angry at the whites or to make isolated individuals responsible. On the whole the employees are well looked after'.[51] On the land issue, too, they compromised: after the government had resumed the land one missionary wrote that 'even if the natives will not forget the loss of their land quickly, they will still gain advantages from the whites'.[52] Labour and land were two matters on which the missionaries should never have given way, and they should have been prepared to admit that any benefits coming to the people from European exploitation of their lands and labour were at best marginal. Perhaps it was correct for the missionaries to attempt to live on good terms with the townspeople and to seek out their company, but they may not have realized what effect this might have on the villagers. The more they fraternized with other, secular Europeans, the less difference the people could see between them all. In aligning themselves with the townspeople they were demonstrating to the villagers the unity of the white settlers. Now the people could see that the mission was but one of the many faces of the West; it thus became easier for them to dismiss the mission as simply one more part of the Western culture that was intruding on their own.

Although the people may have been prepared to dismiss the mission, they retained their loyalty to particular missionaries. Thus Schmutterer was never rejected personally, though Maurer may have been. When Schmutterer retired prematurely because of ill health in 1935, the people grieved for him as if he had died. He had been in Lae for twenty-four years and in that time they had grown to love and respect him as father figure and repository of all Christian wisdom and virtue. His sudden departure was a shock to them and many could not adjust easily to his replacement. Maurer discovered this as soon as Schmutterer had gone: he reported that

> in the first part of the year the congregation was completely over-come by sorrow ... Sometimes an elder of the congregation would come and stand on the verandah and do nothing but wail, 'Oh, Schmutterer! Oh, Schmutterer!' The next part of the year was marked by the fact that in everything I thought of they would say, 'Schmutterer did it like this'.[53]

Although Maurer had expected some reaction against his appoint-ment, he was disappointed by the lack of co-operation he obtained, by the slowness with which he gained the confidence of the people, and by their failure to respond to his requests. The people clearly viewed their Christian duty in much the same way as they had seen the obligations of the traditional religion, that is as a reciprocal relationship with a particular person, in this case Schmutterer. It was he rather than Maurer who had brought them peace and a release from the burdens of traditional religion; in addition he had given them education and access to Western material goods, and had cured their diseases, nursed them, consoled them and defended them against other Europeans. In short they had a duty towards him which they did not feel towards Maurer; Maurer was simply a new-comer whom they did not know and who had achieved nothing for them.

Because they felt no obligation to him, Maurer could not expect to rely merely on his authority as a missionary. But this is what he tended to do, and as a result he simply alienated large numbers of his congregation. Schmutterer had matured among the Lae and knew his people well; but Maurer was young and in his brash enthusiasm made a number of errors which the former missionary would never have made. His insistence that the coastal villages should furnish the evangelists with brides was one error. Another was his readiness to withhold the sacraments of baptism and communion for compara-tively trivial offences—something to which Schmutterer resorted only rarely as a punishment for the most serious offences. His habit of closing the Ampo church from time to time in an effort to stir up enthusiasm for evangelism was yet another mistake. The congrega-tion was proud of their church because they had built it and paid for it themselves, and it was one of the largest buildings around the

Huon Gulf. It is an imposing structure built to seat seven hundred
people. It had been consecrated only in 1933 and had been the crown-
ing achievement of Schmutterer's ministry. It had been opened
amidst great ceremony in the presence of a crowd of local villagers,
numerous visitors from neighbouring congregations, a deputation of
fifty Europeans who had taken the unusual action of coming over
from Lae for the ceremony, and the mission director from Australia,
Dr F. O. Theile. (The Ampo church, along with the Guinea Airways hangar, was one of the few buildings in Lae that survived the
war relatively undamaged. It is now the only pre-war building in
Lae, as the Guinea Airways hangar was dismantled in 1969.) The
congregation looked to their church as a monument to their own
efforts, to the strength of their Christian faith, and to the fact that
they were the foundation and the centre of the Lae mission district.
Shutting it may have shocked them into an initial display of zeal, but
could not have served to maintain their enthusiasm for long. In the
years before World War II Maurer's protests about the lackadaisical
attitude of his congregation grew more frequent and bitter. He wrote
to his superiors that he had 'never seen so much indifference and
laziness and so little striving after goals as here'.[54] He took stern
measures to shake the people up, but they continued to drift away
from him and his mission. It was his failing that he could not appreciate the real reasons for this.

The people later returned to Christianity. After the Japanese
invasion had swept away most of the missionaries and all of the
townspeople, they rediscovered their need for Christianity and kept
their faith alive without the help of missionaries. The missionaries
had not thought that this would be possible; they had been too paternalistic to realize that the people were capable of such independent
action. One of them, for example, had once written that 'it would be
a great pity if the congregation was without the ordering hand of a
white man. The blacks have the good will but little talent for the
orderliness of the white';[55] and another had said, 'they are not able
to discipline themselves and are not able to create order'.[56] The missionaries had closer dealings, more detailed knowledge, and a longer
association with the villagers than any other Europeans, but in the
final analysis they were but another facet of Western culture. They
opposed the materialism of the town and offered the spirituality of
Christianity in its place, yet their requirements were essentially the
same as those of other townspeople, for they were demanding the
loyalty of the people to an imported culture. In the end the main

difference between the two aspects of Western culture, spiritual and temporal, was the degree to which the former had been grafted upon the village society.

A withdrawal from Western influence?

The Europeans, both missionaries and townspeople, may not have realized it, but in the final years before World War II, the behaviour of the village people showed that they were becoming wearied by the encroachments the West was making on their society, that the various influences of European culture were having a depressing effect on them. It is hard to determine now exactly what they thought of white men, but there were signs that they were beginning to reject Europeans and were attempting to withdraw from their influence.

For the villagers the loss of all their lands between the Markham and the Bumbu was the bitterest experience they had in their dealings with Europeans and the one they resented the most. It has remained an ulcerous sore in the relationship between the villagers and the townspeople and will probably remain so until the issue is settled to their satisfaction.[57] At first the people were too timid to seek redress because they were in great awe of the government and white men generally: as one of their *tultuls*, Ahi Yomkwa, said, 'Unimportant men cannot talk with the *kiap*. If unimportant men spoke to the *kiap* they would annoy him and he would gaol them'.[58] After the airstrip had been cleared and they saw beyond doubt that they had lost their land, they summoned enough courage to go to a *kiap* who was in town at the time and raised the matter of compensation with him. This was probably about 1930. The *kiap* came into the village to discuss the matter with them, but they got little satisfaction because they were not recompensed, the government seemed to take no more interest, and the town continued to expand. Early in 1937 they made another attempt to gain compensation. This time they approached Judge B. Montagu Phillips, who was in Lae aboard the government yacht, *Franklin*. Two Butibam men, Ahi Yomkwa and Ahi Naundu, went aboard to put their case to him. He promised to investigate their claims on his return to Rabaul. (Phillips had already heard a number of native land claims on the Gazelle Peninsula and was sympathetic to New Guineans). Shortly after his departure from Lae the volcanic eruptions of May 1937 caused such havoc in Rabaul that their request was probably overlooked, and nothing further happened in their case until 1953 when they raised the issue with a United Nations visiting mission. In the meantime the loss of their land continued to anger them. The knowledge that European settlement was permanent and that their attempts to seek redress had achieved nothing left them with a deep sense of injustice and resentment against Europeans. Their frustration at not knowing the proper ways and means of gaining compensation and in knowing that they did not have the strength to command the respect of Europeans in order to gain a just settlement aggravated their feelings of bitterness. It gave them good reason for turning their backs on Europeans.

European attitudes to New Guineans gave them further cause to reject white men. Relations between New Guineans in pre-war New Guinea were based on the assumption that the Europeans had the inalienable right to command, to be called 'master', while the New Guinean was a 'boy' who had the duty to obey.[59] There is much evidence to show that these assumptions governed race relations in Lae as in other places. The sweated labour demanded of New Guineans, the minimal medical treatment given to them, the racialist names—'coon', 'kanaka', 'boong'—contemptuously applied to them, all showed that the whites did not place much value on New Guineans as a race. So did the general amusement among Europeans at the simplicity of the New Guineans and their confusion in the face of Western technological superiority. The pilot who related after one of his flights that 'when the kanakas saw me gripping the controls they concluded I was holding the machine in the air and declared I was "strongfeller too much" '[60] probably raised a laugh in the bar, but the New Guineans who may have overheard him probably realized that he thought they, too, were stupid.

What New Guineans thought of Europeans is more difficult to determine. Perhaps they accepted the inferior position to which Europeans assigned them,[61] but although they may have accepted arrogance of white men, they were probably hurt by it, for it negated their value as human beings and undermined their self-esteem. No record survives to show what the Lae villagers thought of the Europeans' assumptions of superiority, though a note left by one of the missionaries indicates that they may have resented it: in 1933 soon after the arrival of the first Chinese he noted that the Chinese storekeepers were popular among the villagers because they 'gave their customers consideration' the people were not used to receiving from the Europeans.[62] 'The yellow man has patience', the missionary observed, 'he smiles and does not want to be more than the *Nga'mala**. This gives him an immense amount of power over the naive natives. Why shouldn't they be attracted to him? He is intimately involved with them'.[63] Doubtless the Chinese wanted just as much from the New Guinean as the white man did but he was more subtle in his approach, and as a result the people found in the Chinese an expatriate who did not regard them with contempt or treat them patronizingly. They felt a warm regard for the Chinese which they did not have for the Europeans and later, during the Pacific War, they showed their liking by sheltering them and providing for them during the Japanese occupation. In turning to the Chinese they were turning away from the Europeans, both missionaries and townspeople, and their reason was the dignity which the Chinese accorded them.

Throughout the 1930s Europeans who had close dealings with the Lae complained of an attitude among the people which was variously described as 'lethargy', 'apathy' or 'fatalism'. As early as 1930 Schmutterer had remarked on this aspect of their response to him: 'Their good will comes into conflict with their lack of energy all the time. On top of this comes a lack of judgement and responsibility which is almost a type of fatalism. If their first attempt does not succeed they usually give up. One always has to give them new direction and goals'.[64] Maurer was complaining of something similar when he observed that 'there is a great deal of laziness here, and so it happens that when the missionary is away the Sunday service itself is cancelled'.[65] To the missionaries it seemed that only their presence prevented the people from sinking into total inaction. In pointing to the indifference of the Lae the missionaries usually compared them unfavourably with the Labu. The Lae were usually depicted as being lazy and inactive, whereas their neighbours from across the Markham were supposed to be enthusiastic and vibrant. The missionaries do not seem to have considered the possibility that the difference between the two groups was a function of the isolation of the Labu from the town rather than of some inherent defect among the Lae.

Perhaps the lack of enthusiasm the missionaries found in the villages around the town can be related to the prolonged and intense contact they had had with Europeans. In the decades since Europeans had first settled among them, they had experienced a bewilder-

* *Nga'mala* is the Yabem word for village man.

ing number of changes. They had given their loyalty to the
missionaries, the first Europeans to live among them, and had seen
the supremacy of the mission challenged and toppled by government officials and employers. They had been over-recruited for
contract labour and exceptional demands had been made on them
for day labour in the town. They had lost their prime land for the
building of the aerodrome and the town, and in the face of white
man's law backed by his unassailable power they had been unable to
halt this. There had been the unsettling experience of the rapid build-
up of European settlement at a time when they were being exposed to
the full power of European technology during the Lae–Bulolo airlift.
The departure of their most trusted European, Schmutterer, came at
a critical time when they were beginning to suspect that the mission
had turned against them. They found that the strict morality of the
mission was increasingly difficult to follow and were having trouble
with the roles to which the missionaries had assigned them. There
had been the continuing demoralizing epidemics, against which even
the power of the white men seemed ineffectual. They had been told
that their old beliefs and values were damnable heathenism. They
had been treated as inferiors and had come to expect abuse and
derision from most Europeans. Finally, much of their traditional
social fabric had decayed as their elders were rejected, their women
prostituted, and their young people seduced by the material attractions of the town. Amidst these bewildering experiences they probably had difficulty in maintaining a sense of direction and it is
possible that they became sceptical and suspicious of European
efforts to arouse them. It is also possible that their apparent apathy
was not simply a sign of laziness, or even of bewilderment. It may
have been a refuge for them, a bland exterior they deliberately
assumed while assessing the demands being made on them. If in fact
it was but a protective guise, then they were certainly more sophisti-
cated than any European might have cared to admit.

There is strong reason to suspect that by the time the Japanese
invasion drove out the Europeans, the villagers were thoroughly
disillusioned with the West. Many aspects of their behaviour can be
read as showing that they wished to resist Europeans. Their efforts
to be recompensed for the loss of their land hinted at a growing
militancy which developed further after the war. The revival of
elements of pagan religion in some families possibly meant that they
could no longer accept the beliefs imposed by Western science and
religion and that they wished to return to a system of beliefs which

they could understand. The warmth of their regard for the Chinese may have been a sign that they resented the superiority of Europeans and wished to be treated as human beings. Their resistance against the marriage patterns the missionaries wished to enforce indicated that they objected to European interference with their socio-economic system. The persistent moral transgression and the mounting dissatisfaction among their mission workers suggested that they could no longer play the roles prescribed for them by Europeans. And finally, their reluctance to assist in inland mission extension demonstrated their rejection of what they believed was the denigration of their coastal culture. Did these signs together show that the Lae villagers were wearied by the process of Westernization, that they were repudiating Europeans and their society, that they wished to return to their old ways? Because none of them articulated or recorded their innermost thoughts at the time, such questions are now difficult to answer. There is much to suggest, however, that at least they wished to be left alone by whites, to pursue their own interests in their own time.

No matter what they thought of Europeans and regardless of how much they longed for the simple village life, they were to find that they could not turn back the pages of history. Too much had been lost and what remained was irretrievably altered. The old social order had disintegrated because of the release of the younger generation and its unwillingness to submit to traditional authority. Increasing marriage outside of the village community was beginning to blur old alliances and relationships. They could not return to the old religion because so much of it had been lost and Christianity had been too firmly implanted. Nor could they reject the mission entirely, for it continued to sustain them, and the missionaries, however misguided, were so deeply concerned with their welfare that a bond remained between them. Their close proximity to Lae prevented them from withdrawing physically and meant that they would always have close relations with the town, so that a substantial body of them had to be urban wage-earners rather than subsistence gardeners. Moreover the loss of their lands meant reduced garden space, with the result that any future increase in population had to be absorbed into the town rather than the village economy. All of this meant that the villagers had to compromise with European settlement rather than reject it.

The war years later made astounding demands on the people. Much of their garden land was temporarily laid waste and their homes destroyed. They were uprooted by the Japanese and Australian-American invasions and spent the war years fleeing from one part of their district to another to avoid being harassed by soldiers and blasted by bombs. But despite its turmoil and confusion the war was also a time of respite for the people: with the influence of the Europeans temporarily withdrawn they could see their problems and needs in perspective and were able to attempt a new synthesis to take them into the post-war years.

7

WAR AND POST-WAR

The Lae villagers survived the first impact of white settlement and the foundation of a town within their midst. They also survived the Pacific War and the post-war reconstruction and growth of the town, which has now become a city. Whether they can maintain their separate identity as the city expands around and beyond them is uncertain. The people are conscious of this danger and have begun organizing themselves to avert it.

The Pacific War

The war devastated Lae. Only a few buildings were intact at its end, including the Ampo church and the Guinea Airways hangar. It also ravaged the local villages and made refugees of the people, who were forced to lead a miserable, nomadic existence for four years in order to keep away from the savage bombing and shooting which tore up their homelands as the fighting see-sawed between the Japanese and the Allies. At first they had abandoned their villages and fled into the bush to escape the Japanese bombing, but later they returned and lived on fairly amicable terms with the Japanese, who they did not welcome but did not actively oppose.[1] Possibly they displayed the same apathy that had been apparent in their dealings with Europeans in the pre-war period, and assumed a mask of indifference to shield themselves from the demands of the invaders. The Japanese largely left them to themselves once their neutrality and deference to Nippon had been established beyond doubt. As one villager recalls: 'They instructed us to bow down to them and say "Ohayu" whenever they arrived to inspect us and to bow and say "Sayonara" when they departed. And so we just got used to bowing and saying "Sayonara" '.[2]

The Japanese did, however, cause anxious moments for some villagers because their presence brought a crisis of loyalties. The people knew that the war was a struggle between the Axis powers and the Allies and they had friends on each side: the mission staff mostly had comprised Germans, who had been interned in Australia, but there had also been numbers of Americans and Australians. Each side, Japanese and Allies, demanded the loyalty of the people and was suspicious of those who remained neutral or seemed to have supported the other side. The predicament of people caught between the two camps like this can be seen in the case of Nagong Gejammec of Butibam, the teacher in charge of the Ampo school, and T. of Wagang, who became a guide for the Japanese. When the Japanese entered the Ampo school for the first time they accused Gejammec of being an agent of the Australians and Americans:

> 'Huh, you're just a teacher for the Australians and Americans!' they told me. 'No, I'm a New Guinean teacher and I only know about my own country. I haven't any pupils from Australia or America or anywhere else; they're just New Guineans from this area, and I'm a New Guinean too and this is my village'. They said many things like that to me and I could see that things were not going to be pleasant.[3]

As a result Gejammec and his pupils left Ampo and set up their school in the foothills on the far side of the Busu. Here they were relatively free from interference and could escape into the jungle whenever the Japanese approached, but not all were able to remain neutral or to withdraw into the Busu foothills. A number of the men were impressed as guides and carriers by the Japanese and their co-operation with the invaders later got them into trouble after the return of the Australians. The case of T. indicates the way in which such men could be caught up by events. He was the guide for a Japanese patrol that marched up the Markham to Chivasing village to ambush a pair of Australian coast watchers who were known to be operating in the area. As the two men entered the village they were fired on. One escaped, but the other was shot in the hip; T. ran in and clubbed him to death with the butt of his rifle. After the Allied reoccupation T. joined an Australian labour line for a time and when the military authorities began making enquiries about the Chivasing incident he fled down the coast and hid in Waganluhu village. He was later caught there by an Australian patrol guided by the Butibam *tultul* and was brought back to Lae for trial. He was hanged near the beach at Yanga before a crowd of several thousand villagers from around the Huon Gulf and Markham valley. Among the crowd were his wife and young son.[4]

The most terrifying part of the war for the villagers was the bombing, which was particularly intense in the weeks preceding the Allied recapture of Lae in September 1943. The Allies took the precaution beforehand of dropping leaflets over the villages warning the people to move out of the area, and those who got the leaflets fled inland to hide in the hills. The Japanese prepared for the air raids by building a complex system of tunnels beneath Lo'wamung to serve as air-raid shelters. They cut down all the coconut palms in Butibam for roof supports. The villagers, however, had no air-raid shelters and those who had not been quick enough in escaping deep into the jungle experienced a living nightmare, frantically scurrying for cover every time they heard a plane coming over. Occasionally they were not fast enough and a number were killed. One night a family of five was killed when a bomb scored a direct hit on its house. Another constant fear was that they would be caught in the cross-fire between the opposed armies. During the major engagement fought at the mouth of the Busu a large number of people had fled inland to Gwabadek village, but they found a troop of Japanese had also retreated there; realizing that the village could come under fire they fled back towards the coast and decided to wait out the battle in Kamkumung. They had just settled down there when a large force of Japanese entered the village. The Japanese were retreating from the battle at the Busu and many were seriously wounded and unable to walk. Once again the people were afraid of getting involved in the fighting, but as night was coming on they decided not to flee until next morning At about midnight they were startled by the sound of shots, but stayed put. Next morning they discovered that the Japanese had gone but had shot all their soldiers who were unable to walk. 'There were bodies strewn all over the place like bits of firewood', one villager recalls.[5]

Terryifying, destructive and disruptive though it was, the war nevertheless enabled the people to find the bearings they had lost in the pre-war years under the pressure of the rapid growth of a town in their midst. During the war they were able to return to the church and become confirmed in their Christian faith. Thrown on to their own resources they found that Christianity could sustain them and that it gave them the strength to survive the great dislocation of the

war. Once more the congregation became a focus of their group will
and a powerful force for maintaining their corporate indentity. They
managed to keep their school open and to hold regular church services and celebrations throughout the war, thus proving false the
fears of the missionaries who had believed that the withdrawal of
European influence would mean a reversion to paganism. Arnold
Maahs, a Lutheran army chaplain who entered Lae with the American troops, was amazed to find Lutheranism flourishing among the
people. On entering Butibam he found that one of the evangelists,
Philemon Balob, had served as a pastor to the people throughout the
Japanese occupation, while Gejammec had kept the school running
under great difficulty. Philemon had carried out the functions of the
Lutheran missionary faithfully, baptizing, preaching, counselling,
though he had not served Holy Communion since running out of
communion wine.[6] Maahs was so impressed by the way in which
the various coastal congregations had kept Christianity alive that he
wrote a book about his experiences in New Guinea, one of the
chapters of which was 'Butibam keeps the faith alive'. The title he
chose, *Our Eyes Were Opened*, indicated something of the astonish-
ment of white missionaries that the church had survived without the
guiding hand of Europeans. The people, however, did not think
they had done anything unusual: as Gejammec said, 'We decided
that we must keep things going if we were not to return to the ways
of our ancestors; if we did let things drop we would only have a
difficult task of recovery after the war'.[7] The first missionary to
return was Theodore Fricke, who arrived shortly after Maahs. He
called a meeting of elders and found that 'they rejoiced to learn
that their mission had not been forgotten' and would be re-
established immediately.[8] They were glad to have their missionaries
back despite having proved that they could survive without them.

The Allied reoccupation did not mean the end of the war for the
people. Both Americans and Australians concentrated vast forces in
the Lae area in preparation for campaigns further north. Although
the main concentration was at Finschhafen, where there were 700 000
American troops at the height of the build-up, Lae was still an
important base. There were 10 000 Australians and 10 000 Americans
in the town, mostly in support units, with a further 50 000 Americans
quartered at Nadzab, the new airstrip built near the old Gabmatzung mission station. Lae suddenly became a military metropolis of
temporary buildings. Gavin Long, an official Australian war historian, described it as

a fairly comfortable town of considerable size. Along wide, heavily-metalled roads were lines of buildings with concrete or timber floors, walls only half-height to allow the air to circulate, and ceilings of tar board. Neatly painted road signs—Wau Avenue, Finschhafen Avenue and so on—guided the traveller . . . Twice a week there was an open-air picture show, and often films not yet seen on the mainland were shown . . . Five miles away on the banks of the Busu was an officers' club with room for about 200 to dine, served by well-drilled native waiters, and with a fine floor on which officers danced with nurses to music played by a four-man band.[9]

A New Guinean labour force of 3000 was needed to service the town and this was recruited by ANGAU*; as a result most of the able bodied men from local villages now found themselves working for the Allies in much the same way as they had worked in the pre-war town. The remaining villagers were evacuated by ANGAU to make way for military installations, which stretched almost unbroken from the Markham to the Busu. The people were relocated with army assistance on a site called Lo'sang, five miles from Lae on the far side of the Busu, and here they lived for the remainder of the war. They were not able to return to their villages immediately the war ended, for after the war the civilian administration took over the buildings the army had erected, and was reluctant to hand the area back to the people again. The people began moving back to the villages in 1947 but it was not until 1950 that the administration finally gave up the last buildings it was occupying in Butibam. For the people the war thus lasted for nearly a decade; the dislocation it brought during that time will not be easily forgotten.

The post-war reconstruction of the town

In early 1946, with the war barely over, the civilian population of Lae began returning. Among the first to arrive back were the missionaries. They found that the area had changed beyond recognition. Nearly all of the old town had been destroyed and in its place was a vast, sprawling army camp. Their sense of disorientation amidst

* ANGAU: the Australian New Guinea Administrative Unit, a military organization that had the responsibility of administering the civilian population in Allied occupied parts of Papua New Guinea. It was staffed mainly by officers who had lived in pre-war New Guinea and who therefore had 'colonial experience'.

these unfamiliar surroundings can be seen in the first report filed by
the Reverend F. E. Pietz, an American missionary who had been
posted to Lae after Maurer's internment in 1939. On his return he
found that

> the first few weeks were a time of bewilderment. Even on the
> mission station at Ampo I was lost—the old landmarks were gone,
> almost endless army installations covered the area which had been
> so familiar to me, roads had no relation to the old ones, villagers
> were not seen, all old buildings destroyed and their old sites en-
> tirely overgrown. The distance from Lae to Ampo was the same,
> but while I used to tramp over this road on foot—an hour used to
> be my usual time—now trucks and jeeps raced through in a few
> minutes. I felt like a native of New Guinea might feel if he sud-
> denly landed in Brisbane. To get my balance again I found the
> familiar faces of the natives were helpful.[10]

Because nothing remained of the pre-war town, returning townspeople at first occupied the army huts in the area around Butibam, or
Charing Cross as it had become known to army personnel because of
the newly constructed roads that met there. Even the Hotel Cecil,
pride of the pre-war years, had to start up business in Butibam,
operating temporarily from what one visitor described as a 'prepos-
terous caravanserai of rotting grass huts'.[11] The town and its citizens
thus faced a lengthy and time-consuming task of reconstruction.

Returning townspeople found that they had more to cope with
than an unfamiliar physical setting, for the war had brought other
changes as well. They were irritated to find that the old assumptions
about white supremacy and black subservience were no longer
accepted by the New Guineans. In early 1947 the Lae correspondent
of the *Pacific Islands Monthly* reported that 'the young native lad in
his teens at the outbreak of the war contacted many of our troops
with leftist ideas and was treated lavishly. At the same time the
young native cultivated, as a result of these casual contacts, a superior
tolerance of the white race as a whole'.[12] He went on to state his
opinion that the 'war adolescents' were preparing to evict Europeans
from New Guinea and said that 'the presence of thousands of rounds
of ammunition, rifles and war equipment hidden in the villages does
not tend to make the situation any easier'[13] Another old Lae hand
was horrified to find that Lae had become a place 'where white men
work'.[14] She said that 'the old myth that manual labour in New
Guinea is an excursion ticket to the cemetery has been exploded.

White men *do* work—and hard— and the death rate has not gone up'.[15] Even white women had to work: 'It is no longer *infra dig* for Madame Territorian to do her own housework. She will if she can of course still rely on native servants, though they are more unreliable and undisciplined than previously'.[16] Obviously the New Guineans were no longer prepared to accept inferior status, nor did they believe it was obligatory for them to supply their services to the Europeans. The war had liberated them from their pre-war subservience.

The old town was not rebuilt and the site for the new Lae was shifted from the flat foreshore land between Voco Point and the aerodrome to the terraces above where in pre-war days only the town's elite had lived, physically as well as socially prominent. Nor did Lae retain its capital status: with the union of Papua and New Guinea that prize went to Port Moresby. Lae did, however, get a consolation prize as the headquarters of the Morobe District in place of Salamaua, which had been bombed into extinction and has never been rebuilt. The new Lae, which has been built according to a town plan drawn up in 1949, is well planned and picturesque. It developed in a northerly direction across the river terraces rather than along the flats near the aerodrome as the old town had done. At the same time a new light-industrial area opened up in the Milfordhaven area on the far side of the aerodrome towards the Markham mouth. This area was strongly oriented towards the new wharf, which the Americans had built during their period of occupation. The Milfordhaven pier became the main overseas wharf, whereas the pre-war harbour at Asiawe near Voco Point became the terminal for local shipping and small boats. The new town soon developed facilities that the old town had lacked—churches, shops, a hospital, a school for European children—and has become a garden town of scenic shaded avenues and neat bungalows. Its attractions are now its spacious parks and reserves, the most notable of which are the botanical gardens and war cemetery; a visit to these has become a feature on the itinerary of tourist excursions to New Guinea.

The impression that the new Lae is an expatriate town is strong, though appearances are deceptive. One scholar who has studied its growth has observed that like most other Pacific port towns Lae is 'the creation of alien influences'.[17] He has pointed out that 'there are no urban traditions among the indigenes. Lae therefore owes its existence and subsequent growth to European enterprise'.[18] That of course is true, but it is not the whole truth for it overlooks the role of

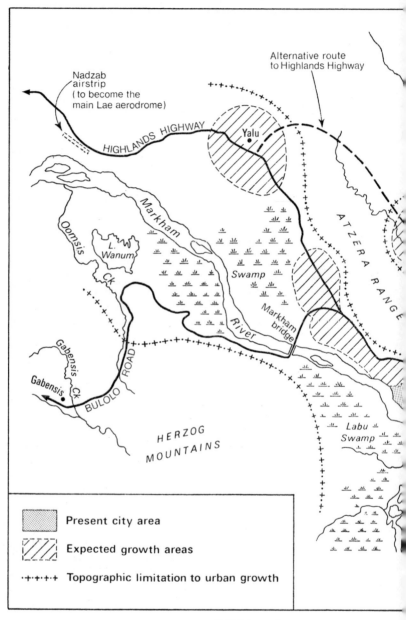

Long-range growth possibilities for Lae

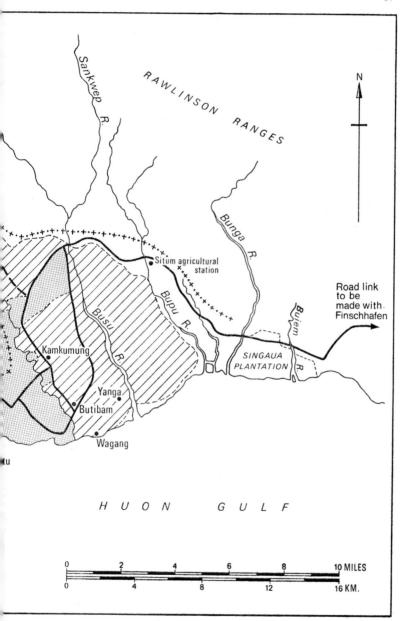

the indigenous community in the town. Although the urban area was originally the creation of Europeans, the experience of people like the Lae villagers shows that indigenous villages on the town fringes are deeply involved in the urbanizing process and have a close association with urbanization over a long period. They are deeply affected by the growth of the town and they make a notable contribution to its development, even though they are not the instigators or prime-movers. Furthermore it is becoming obvious that the New Guineans are no longer prepared to be the same mute, unobtrusive and compliant body they were in the pre-war town. They are now the overwhelming majority of the population and in recent years have begun to assert their power in a number of directions. A rising militancy became apparent as Papua New Guinea's final drive towards political independence accelerated during 1971, 1972 and 1973. This was seen in a number of successful industrial strikes organized by the local indigenous Workers' Association after 1971 and also in the success of Pangu Pati, a political party with strong roots in Lae, in mobilizing the indigenous population to get its candidates returned at the city council and parliamentary elections. The New Guineans are clearly taking an initiative in public affairs in Lae and will certainly demand an increasingly larger say in the future development of the city. As they do the expatriate domination of city affairs will perhaps decline.

Post-war growth

Lae has grown steadily in the post-war period, although it took some time to get going because of the depressed state of the economy in the immediate post-war years. The population by 1949–50 was about 1400 and this grew to about 10 000 by 1963–4. Its main function was administrative and it served as the headquarters for both the Morobe District and the New Guinea mainland region. As late as 1964, 50 per cent of the expatriate population and 40 per cent of the indigenes worked in the public sector, either for the administration or for Australian government departments.[19] Industrial enterprise was confined to sawmilling, the manufacture of beverages, and wharfage and storage. The latter became important after 1954 when a plywood industry was established in Bulolo by a consortium of the gold mining companies and the Commonwealth government. This industry depended on the Milfordhaven wharf and on the Wau–

Bulolo–Lae road, which had finally been pushed through during the war.

After 1965 Lae moved into its current stage of rapid expansion during which it has achieved city status and has become the second largest urban area in Papua New Guinea after Port Moresby. The impetus for this was the completion of the Highlands Highway linking Lae with the agriculturally rich highlands region between Kainantu and Mount Hagen. The effect of this new transport connection was to lower freight rates and thus draw cargo movements between the coast and highlands away from air transport based on Madang. Before the completion of the highway any cargo—building materials, machinery, vehicles, fuel, food supplies—going to the highlands had to be shipped to Madang, the nearest coastal port, and then air-freighted in at considerable expense. Thus as a result of the completion of the highway the total tonnages of shipping cargoes handled at Lae (excluding normal intra-territory cargoes) increased at an annual rate of 26 per cent between 1963–4 and 1968–9, that is, more than threefold over the five-year period. By contrast the rate of increase for Papua New Guinea as a whole was only half that figure.[20] The improved access between Lae and the highlands had an immediate impact on commercial and industrial activity in Lae. The town soon became the most important centre for road transport in the country and this stimulated the growth of manufacturing industries to serve the newly opened highlands market, which contains nearly 40 per cent of the national population; this in turn led to an expansion of industries and commercial services already established in the town, particularly building construction, retailing, and finance. 'Not only has Lae benefited from the diversion of existing traffic movements to it', an urban development study has found, 'but also it has gained from the general impetus which the improved transport facilities have given to economic development in the highlands'.[21] Among the new industries which came to Lae as a result have been an abattoir and factories for making nails, fabricated wire, steel fencing posts, concrete pipes and bricks, industrial gases and chemicals, bottles, cardboard cartons, metal containers, and paints, and a small iron foundry. Industries about to be established are cement making and match manufacturing. Older industries that have greatly expanded are timber milling, beverages, vehicle and heavy plant assembly and maintenance, coffee milling, building and allied trades, printing, fuel storage and despatch, wharfage and storage. As a result Lae soon outstripped Madang and Rabaul, which had earlier been bigger, so that now it 'is second only to Port Moresby as an industrial centre; and it has been forecast that by 1973 it will have surpassed the latter town in this respect'.[22]

The effect of the sudden industrial and commercial growth has been to make Lae a strong magnet for migration from the surrounding rural districts. By the time of the 1966 census the population had reached about 16 500 and by the 1971 census it numbered about 34 700, an increase of 109.7 per cent, as can be seen from this table:

Population of Lae, 1966 and 1971[23]

	Indigenous			Other			Total		
	Male	Female	Total	Male	Female	Total	Male	Female	Total
1966	8925	4416	13341	1868	1337	3205	10793	5753	16546
1971	18156	10338	28494	3385	2820	6205	21541	13158	34699
Growth (per cent)	103·4	134·1	113·6	81·2	111	93·6	99·6	128·7	109·7

The annual growth rate is high, in the order of 10 per cent, so it is probable that the population at present (1973) is approaching 42 000 and that this rate of increase will be maintained until 1990 at least; if it is, the population will have grown to 47 000 by 1975, to about 100 000 by 1983, and to 195 000 by 1990.[24] Most of the increase has been and will continue to be within the indigenous section of the community. At present Papua New Guineans comprise more than 82 per cent of the population and projections show that by 1990 they will comprise at least 92 per cent.[25]

As a result of this migration Lae has become relatively cosmopolitan in comparison with the pre-war town, and is now a city of Papua New Guinea rather than a town of the Morobe District alone. In addition to peoples from all over the Morobe District there are now substantial colonies of migrants from other districts: Milne Bay, Kerema, Central, Madang, the Sepik, and more recently the Eastern Highlands and Chimbu districts. The first of the migrant communities settled themselves in Lae in the early post-war years. Many of them had come to the town as labourers for ANGAU, working on construction jobs, the wharf and at carrying for the army. After the war they stayed on and assimilated into the urban community. Thus there is a large settlement of people from the area surrounding Kerema in the Papuan Gulf who are now effectively New Guineans, despite their residence in the large suburb behind the wharf known formally as Milfordhaven and informally as the 'Papuan Compound'. Similarly a large colony of Sepik people have settled along the east bank of the Bumbu near the river mouth. Built close to the water, their houses closely resemble the houses along the big river of their home district; many of their number are busily employed carving, for the tourist trade, the wooden masks that have made their home district famous. A newer element are the short, stocky and aggressive migrants from the highland districts that were opened up only after the war. The highway connection has made it easy for them to get to Lae and now thousands of highland people pour into the city each year to find work and enjoy the bright lights.

As more migrants arrive the city is experiencing many of the growth pains of urbanization experienced by other developing nations: the growth of squalid, unplanned migrant settlements; problems with unskilled and unemployed urban drifters; a rise in petty crime; failure to keep up the supply of essential services such as roads, water, sewerage, power and transport; housing and land short-ages; and great pressure on health and educational services. The government through various departments and agencies, most not-ably Social Development and Home Affairs, Adult Education, Business Development, the Housing Commission, and Agriculture, Stock and Fisheries, is endeavouring to cope with these growth problems and receives the active support of the churches and volun-tary organizations. One of the most interesting attempts to relieve a number of the various urban problems has been the establishment of planned migrant settlements under the aegis of the Department of Social Development and Home Affairs. The largest of these is at 'Two Mile', out along the Markham road. It is a settlement of some 3000 people from many parts of the Morobe District and Papua New Guinea. Each settler is given a block of land 50 feet by 100 feet for a nominal rent ($2 per year). The government puts in minimal roads and drainage and the settler erects his own house and is free to upgrade it as he finds the money and materials. To prevent enclaves of tribal groups from developing no settler may obtain a block along-side that of a man from his home area. The settlement has its own primary school and a large community centre containing an assembly hall where public meetings and services of worship may be held, a medical aid post and conference rooms for groups such as women's and youth clubs. It is hoped that settlements such as 'Two Mile' will give the migrants a sense of pride and of belonging to the urban community to counter the negative feelings of alienation and loss of identity that are common among the inhabitants of many rapidly developing cities. In addition to the planned settlements at places such as 'Two Mile' and the 'Papuan Compound', there are a number of expanding Housing Commission estates, such as Huonville near Chinatown and Omili near Kamkumung, where neat, though small, houses have been built for the growing urban middle class of Papua New Guinean white-collar workers: clerks, teachers, shop assistants, professional workers and skilled tradesmen. However, a large sector of the urban indigenous population—more than a third[26]—lives in neither planned settlement nor housing estate. The people of this group are the so-called 'squatters', generally unskilled and uneducated migrants from many parts of the country, who live in a series of sprawling, unsightly camps around the edges of the city. One of the largest of these is the Bumbu settlement on the eastern bank of the river near the former village site at Buko. Here perhaps 8000 people from the upper Markham, the Finschhafen hinterland, the Madang and Sepik districts, the Siassi islands and the Huon Gulf coast are crowded together in a waterlogged, unsanitary shanty town of jumbled, makeshift dwellings. There are few amenities, little privacy, and not much hope for an improved living standard in Buko. From such areas come the unskilled labour on which the city depends for many of its functions, and it is to such places that most rural migrants in search of a cash wage gravitate, to live as a burden on *wantoks** already established there.

While the residential areas, settlement, estate and squatter camp flourish, Lae has also acquired a number of new institutions that are serving to broaden the character and function of the town. Among them are the major teachers' college of the Lutheran education system, Balob, situated in the grounds of Ampo and founded in 1965, and the major Lutheran theological school, the Martin Luther Seminary, founded in 1971 on the site of the old Malahang plantation. In addition, the Igam base of the Pacific Islands Regiment was established in 1968 in the same year that the Papua New Guinea Institute of Technology was transferred from Port Moresby to Lae. During 1973 the Institute was raised to university status and became the nation's second university, taking the name Papua New Guinea University of Technology. In addition to the university, the teachers'

---

* *Wantok* is the Pidgin word for the member of one's tribal, that is linguistic, group. Literally 'one talk' or 'of the same language'. It is also used to indicate friendship; thus *gutpela wantok bilong mi* means 'my mate, my companion'.

college, and the seminary, there are a number of other educational institutions: two technical colleges, four high schools, and twelve primary schools run by the government and the churches. As in most cities the size of Lae there is a wide range of organizations, sporting and social clubs, service clubs, voluntary welfare organizations such as YWCA and Red Cross, churches of many denominations, learned societies, trade unions and political parties, catering for the various needs of the inhabitants. Many of these up till now have been dominated by Europeans and Chinese; whether this will continue after independence is uncertain. Perhaps the most important institution as far as the Papua New Guinean population is concerned is the produce market in Aircorps Road behind the aerodrome. It is open six days a week and is patronized by thousands daily. It serves as a social centre as well as market, and a visit there is perhaps the best means a Papua New Guinean has for meeting his *wantoks*. These various organizations and institutions have brought into Lae a large and diverse population of both indigenes and expatriates and have made it a diverse city.

In contrast to the pre-war and post-war towns, Lae now fulfills all the varied functions of a moderately large commercial and industrial centre. R. B. Rofe, a geographer who has concerned himself with Lae's development, doubted that this was so when he made a close study of the town in 1964. He typified Lae as 'an incipient urban centre' because he believed it had not reached a stage of growth where it contained a population large enough to attract further industry and services.[27] What may have been true in 1964 is no longer true now, for in the last decade the population has more than quadrupled, so that the city has now reached the point of take-off and is large enough to sustain its own future growth. Rofe did concede that Lae was 'culturally generative' because it provided 'many and varied cross-cultural contacts between Western and indigenous cultures'.[28] This function of the city seems likely to receive continued and increasing emphasis. Not only are there Chinese and Europeans of almost every nationality—Australians, British, Americans and Canadians, Hungarians, Turks, Italians and French—there are small numbers of migrants from other areas: West Indians, Ceylonese, Indians, Filipinos, Indonesians, Japanese and Tongans. All these groups may be expected to enrich the quality of contacts with the hundreds of Papua New Guinean ethnic groups in Lae. As the country emerges from colonial dependency and seeks new bearings during its first years of independence, a wave of nationalism may be expected to arise and sweep away many of the barriers that once separated cultures and races, though of course new barriers may be erected in their place.

In 1972 Lae became Papua New Guinea's second city on the request of its first urban council, which was elected in April 1971.[29] The second city council was elected in April 1973 and leadership of the council has been captured by the Papua New Guineans, who combined without consideration of party affiliation to defeat European and Chinese candidates for the positions of Lord Mayor and Deputy Lord Mayor. The Lord Mayor is a medical orderly who comes from the Sepik and his deputy, a foreman from the Public Works Department, comes from Port Moresby. The new council has a difficult task ahead of it. As the country gains independence and nationhood there will be a certain amount of dislocation that will be felt first in the cities. A number of expatriate public servants will depart and there will be a difficult transitional period as the Papua New Guineans who take their places acquire the necessary experience and skill. There are, of course, numerous prophets of doom who write pessimistic letters to the national daily newspaper, the *Post-Courier* (which now brings out a special Lae edition) warning of impending disaster. Unsettled conditions as the changeover to independence takes place may persuade a number of expatriate businessmen to pack up and go and if they do there will be some dislocation in the provision of goods and services and in employment until their places are taken either by indigenous entrepreneurs or by new investors from abroad, such as the Japanese, who are at present showing lively interest in New Guinea. The city council has strong business representation and will possibly see a major part of its role as a need to reassure businessmen in order to maintain their confidence in the future of the city and thus to guarantee employment opportunities. At the same time it will have to balance that aspect of its task against the rising aspirations of the indigenous community, which will make increasing demands for the services the council is bound to provide: roads and footpaths, street lighting, water, sewerage, transport, power, and recreational, health and educational facilities. At the same time the rapid expansion of the urban area beyond the present city boundaries and into the rural areas outside will cause problems with the villagers for the council. A major urban development study of Lae's future development has recommended that new industrial and residential areas be established on the present village lands outside the city boundaries.[30] The villagers, however, are suspicious of the city and will probably oppose any move that looks like bringing them under the wing of the city council. As a result dealings with the village community are going to be one of the council's greatest headaches. Lae seems certain to become one of the great cities of the Pacific but it will experience considerable travail before it achieves that pre-eminence.

The village community

While the city has flourished on the opposite bank of the Bumbu the five traditional villages appear to have stood still. Despite their proximity to the city they have not yet been assimilated into it and are still a separate entity. The village houses, often built from re-claimed scraps of timber, iron and fibro-cement, seem dilapidated even by comparison with the houses in the adjacent 'squatter' camps. They stand in strong contrast to the neat bungalows of the city and to the other traditional villages to east and west where houses are still built of native materials and have a neat, post-card picturesqueness. The people are aware of this and it makes them self-conscious and defensive. One of the village elders in Butibam, Kamdring Bukaua, showed this when, in welcoming the Acting Morobe District Commissioner into the village in 1972, he said

> Living so close to Papua New Guinea's second city, it shames us when outsiders come into our village. Our living conditions are just like those of our ancestors in spite of our efforts to catch up with the social and economic changes that are taking place around us. If you don't mind our living conditions and if you are interested in helping us change them, come in.[31]

Part of the Lae villagers' problem is that they are next to the city but not of it. Most of the village women and older men tend gardens, and garden produce is an important part of their food supply. Most of the younger men and many of the young women have jobs in the town, though the villagers are disappointed that their young people have not been successful in securing places in the tertiary training institutions and that they do not hold important positions in the city —jobs that outsiders always seem to fill. This disappointment is occasionally seen in motions brought before the Huon Council (the municipal organization covering the rural area around Lae, of which the five villages are technically a part) to have certain classes of jobs in the city restricted to local villagers. One of the reasons for the lack of prominence of the villagers in local affairs is a legacy of the Yabem education system—which was well organized and efficient and produced a high level of literacy, but deprived the older villagers (those over forty) of an extensive education in English. Some missions in other districts have taught in English for generations, with the result that their proteges were ready to advance when employment localization schemes began. The Lae have had to wait while a new generation of young people has moved through the English schools, and consequently have had the bitter experience of seeing people from areas where education is more recent out-stripping them in competition for places in the nation's new middle class. Some of the people nurse a resentment and are inclined to blame the mission for their disadvantage.

Although the villages are still intact despite the inroads of a century of European contact and settlement, the people now face a number of pressures which threaten ultimately to fragment their society and to eliminate their separate identity. The encroachment of the town is the strongest of these. It is creeping across the eastern bank of the Bumbu, devouring the village land as it goes. The Bumbu settlement, which first sprang up in 1963 on the old village site at Buko, is now inexorably driving a wedge across the village land between Butibam and Wagang-Yanga. The urban development study recommends that future city growth should be in this direction and then should continue on through the Malahang area into the territory between Butibam and Kamkumung.[32] As this happens the villages will be completely surrounded, becoming tiny islands in a vast urban sprawl. If the people are unable to make satisfactory arrangements for the leasing of their land to the settlers and the industrial entrepreneurs, they could lose the one asset that has done most to draw them together. It seems logical that as the city grows around them they should be included within its boundaries, which stop at the Bumbu at present. Many of them would reject such a development, however, because they want the city to stop at the Bumbu. Their attitude was indicated by Kamdring Bukaua, who expressed a common grievance when he told the town planners, 'Our villagers are short of land. We have told you town planners that you cannot make plans for village land. We want to live according to the custom of our ancestors, and so the town plan must not extend beyond the Bumbu River.'[33] They are aware that if they were absorbed into the city and came under the jurisdiction of its municipal authority, their lands could be made rateable. If that were to happen they would probably find the cost of retaining their property so crippling that they would be forced to sell. This could easily happen if there were a development conscious government in power which wanted to move them out to make way for urban expansion and large-scale industrial development backed by big business from overseas. That, of course, would probably destroy the village society and the people would simply become landless urban dwellers, indistinguishable from other residents around them.

The land remains their chief asset. Although many of them are urban wage earners, their gardens are still important to their food supply, while the sale of this produce supplements wages earned in the city. Evidence for this is the new market, built near Butibam by the villagers in 1972 to facilitate trade in garden produce with the residents of the Huonville Housing Commission estate and the inhabitants of the Bumbu settlement. As the city spreads across the garden lands the people will be deprived of both food supply and supplementary income. The land must therefore be made to yield as much profit through leasing arrangements as will be necessary to offset the loss of their food supply and supplementary income, without which they would be yet another impoverished section of the urban community.

Perhaps the greatest force operating to prevent the Lae from being submerged in the city is their determination to obtain fair treatment in their claims over the land taken from them first by the Neu Guinea Compagnie and then resumed by the government for the establishment of the town. Their deep-seated resentment at what they felt was more than half a century of injustice over the recognition of their land claim has led them to appeal to the United Nations and to sue the government through the courts in an attempt to gain compensation. On three occasions, in 1953, 1956 and 1959 they complained to the United Nations Trusteeship Council Visiting Missions which were touring New Guinea in those years. On the occasion of the 1956 visit they planned a dramatic gesture of protest. The paramount *luluai* of Lae, Kahata Wakang of Ahi-Hengali, stepped before the Mission at a large public meeting and threw an axe and knife on the ground in front of its members and stated that the white man had obtained their land for a paltry sum, which the axe and knife represented. He said that only a few people understood Pidgin at the time the land was taken and no one knew what was happening. They wanted the land back but the government refused to co-operate and would not pay any compensation. The leader of the mission, Sir John Macpherson, referred the complaint to the local administration officials but they were unsympathetic. Their attitude was that the villagers still had ample land left and that the original acquisition was analogous to the purchase of Manhatten Island from the American Indians for a few trinkets.[34] The Lae's continued frustration at being unable to have their claim recognized drove them, in 1971, to the Supreme Court, where they lodged a case for compensation against the government. At this hearing they were granted token compensation only, so they appealed against this decision in 1972 and had the bitter experience of having their appeal rejected. They are still deeply aggrieved and have even considered making an appeal to the High Court of Australia. If the claim is not settled to their satisfaction, the problem will remain and they will be a thorn in the side of the new national government. The government may find it judicious to make a political settlement, such as turning over to them an area of the city at present owned by the government so that they could profit from the high-yielding leases they would control. Their determination to seek adequate redress can be seen in the words of Kamdring Bukaua at a feast given in the village to thank the lawyers who represented the people at their first court hearing:

> Here is a bow and some arrows. They are for you to chase a certain pig with. We have been chasing this old pig for years but he has been very hard to catch. If we do not get him this time we will call out to you again and you can come back, bringing the bow and arrows with you. We will then go hunting together and put a few more arrows into that pig.[35]

This persistence and determination to receive justice in the land case has done much to draw the people together and to preserve their corporate identity. Their wish to safeguard their remaining lands could also prove to be a unifying force.

Encroachments by the city are an external threat to the separate identity of the people, but there are a number of influences within the village society that may also serve to weaken their sense of corporate individuality. One of these dangers is that the village population could become so diluted that it will lose its separate and distinctive character. Outside marriages with people from other districts are now the most common and as a result many outsiders now claim to be Lae villagers. If this trend continues the villages could become mere suburbs with residents of diverse origin and

tenuous kinship links who claim to be villagers. Because of the land
inheritance system of the village society, many outsiders now claim
title to village lands through marriage. It is because of this that rival
religious sects are now making inroads on what has traditionally
been a Lutheran preserve. The villagers, many of whom remain
staunchly faithful to the Lutheran church, oppose the intrusion of
the rival sects. In 1971, for example, the Roman Catholic mission
decided to erect a church in the Bumbu settlement to serve the Sepik
community there; the Butibam people generally regarded this move
as sacrilege because they believe their lands, on which the new
church stands, are hallowed by the Lutheran faith. They bitterly
opposed the Roman Catholic decision but were powerless to prevent
it, as the Sepiks who were responsible were connected through marriage to the lineage owning the land and were able to bring pressure
to bear on the head of the lineage as a result. Similar inroads are also
being made by pentacostalist and fundamentalist sects. Like the land,
the Lutheran church has long been a rallying point for the villagers;
if Lutheranism becomes simply one more religious code among
others, one of the main markers of village identity will have been
lost.

But even their loyalty to the Lutheran church involves certain
dangers for the villagers. In the pre-war period they saw the Kâte
system assume dominance over the Yabem system. Post-war the
trend has continued. Yabem is a minority language and is no longer
taught in the schools, although it has become a second language for
most villagers after Kawa. Pidgin is a third language and is rapidly
replacing Yabem as the liturgical language, and the new European
missionaries now learn Pidgin rather than Yabem. The indigenous
backbone of the Lutheran church in New Guinea is composed of
speakers of Kâte and Pidgin rather than of Yabem. Thus when the
church elected its first indigenous bishop in early 1973 it chose a
pastor from the Kâte area, the Reverend Zure Zurewe, a son of one
of the first Kâte evangelists. The Lutheran church has been a leader
in localizing its positions of responsibility, but the Lae villagers are
suspicious of the Lutheran localization programme. They know that
the Kâte and Pidgin speakers will dominate the autonomous church
and fear that the new leaders may not have as much sympathy for
the coastal culture and the needs of the village community as the
present European officials of the church. The people have a number
of other complaints against the church. They now believe they were
unfairly paid for the mission land at Ampo and Malahang, despite

the fact that the sales were legal and that their forefathers were content with the amount they received. They would secretly like to get the mission lands back and see the mission go elsewhere. The land issue has so deeply embittered them that they could turn against the church. That would be unfortunate, for the church and its white missionaries, despite the changes they wrought upon the village society, have always meant well and have tried to defend and support the people.

Although a number of dangers threaten the village community, there are also a number of influences serving to unite the people and to maintain their separate identity. The claim for compensation in respect of the alienated land is, of course, the chief of these, but there are other influences too. One of the most important is the unanimous opposition of the people to the incursions of the squatters settling around them. Their chief complaints against the squatters are that their number includes an undesirable element of drifters who steal from village gardens, cut down valuable timber and molest the village women and children; a further complaint is that the squatters are allowed to settle on village land provided they pay rents, but once established they tend not to do so and there is no effective machinery for recovering rents that are in arrears. These grievances have accumulated over the years, so that it was not surprising when early in 1972 the people issued warnings to the squatters to quit their lands. Such a massive resettlement would have been necessary if they had carried out their threats that a number of the leaders of the newly formed national government—the Chief Minister, Michael Somare, the Minister for Lands, Albert Maori Kiki, the Minister for Local Government, Boyamo Sali (also the Morobe District Regional representative in parliament), and the local member of parliament, Toni Ila—flew into Lae for urgent consultations with village leaders in an effort to avert the disruptive move. Their pleas were heeded, for the villagers undertook not to evict the squatters for the time being. Nevertheless, the problem of the squatters remains an ugly sore in the relationship between the villagers and the townspeople which is not going to heal easily and will become aggravated when the villagers begin making arrangements for the industrial development of their land, because this will entail large-scale resettlement of the squatters. It is unfortunate that such a negative force should serve to bring the people together, for the related land and squatter issues have produced a siege mentality among some of the people. Their bitterness at having been the victims of history has given some of them such a deep distrust of outsiders, even those missionaries and welfare officers who are closest to them, that they may turn against the people who are in a position to help them. Their hostility to outsiders is revealed in a number of ways. Any driver speeding through a village will be followed by a stream of abuse and perhaps rocks, and anyone crossing village land without permission runs a risk of being set upon. This occasionally leads to major trouble, as in early 1973 when some friends of the Labu were ordered off Ahi-Hengali land near the Markham River bridge. The Labu took this as an insult and came over to Lae to administer a beating to the Ahi-Hengali man who had been responsible. His friends rallied to him and as a result of the riot that followed more than one hundred men from Labu, Ahi-Hengali and Butibam were gaoled.

There are encouraging signs, however, that the people will be able to handle the future pressures and demands of urbanization capably and effectively. The experience they have gained in their land claim and in dealings with lawyers and contacts in the government has taught them that the best chance they have of maintaining their integrity is to be recognized in law as a corporate group. The formation several years ago of the Butibam Progress Association, the village society instrumental in bringing the land claim to court, showed that they understood the need for effective organization to achieve communal ends. But perhaps the most significant recent development within the village community has been the formation of the Ahi Association, a welfare society which was formed in early 1972 to link the five villages and promote and protect their collective interests. Its leaders are a group of ambitious young village men in their twenties and thirties who have had both primary and secondary education in English and who work in the town. They have access to knowledge and professional advice and an understanding of administrative, legal and business procedures which their Yabem educated elders lack. The Ahi Association is rapidly emerging as a vigorous business and political organization and bears many resemblances to the famed Mataungan Association of the Tolai around Rabaul; it has a keen sense of publicity, and on the occasions that it has flexed its muscles has brought attention to itself.

The first issue in which it became obvious that the Ahi Association was strong and well organized was the House of Assembly election for the Lae Open seat in February 1972. The patron of the Association, Steven Ahi, was one of the five candidates and the newly-formed association supported him in a well planned and efficiently-organized campaign. He was unsuccessful, mainly because the large squatter community rallied behind the Pangu Pati banner and voted for the local party leader, Toni Ila. The Association is not regarded favourably by the squatters, who resent the villagers' attitudes towards them. Another issue over which the Association attracted attention was by defying local government officials in going ahead to make its own arrangements for the sale of the Bumbu river gravels to a local building construction firm. Then the Association became involved in a dispute with the city council over the dumping of the city's sanitary and garbage refuse in the Busu River; it rightly asserted that this practice was causing serious pollution of the Busu and was creating a health hazard in Yanga and Wagang as a result. The Association warned the council that it would have to find an alternative site and that if it did not the road into the dumping ground would be sealed off. The council had no alternative but to comply.[36] Early in 1973 the Association opposed the Minister for Trade and Industry, Donatus Mola, over the arrangements he wanted to make with an Australian cement manufacturing company that wished to establish a $10 million cement factory at Wagang. The Wagang people were opposed to the scheme because they feared the pollution that their village might suffer. When Mola publicly criticized the people for their refusal to co-operate, the Association laid the blame at his feet by pointing out that he had not investigated alternative sites offered to him by the Association.[37] Another dispute in which the association is becoming involved results from its suggestion that the five villages should leave the Huon local government council and that the Association itself should be constituted as a recognized local government authority. The squatters, who are the majority of the population within the village area, are opposed to this proposal and would prefer to join the Lae City Council, where their domination by the Association would be modified. They are afraid that if the Association becomes a local government council within its own right the village community would use the council as a weapon against them. The Association, on the other hand, believes that the village lands can be best developed for residential and industrial purposes if a separate council is created.[38]

The Association has ambitious plans for the village lands. In 1973 it secured the assistance of a major building construction company and a firm of town planners to produce the 'Butibam Development Plan', a blueprint for the development of their lands in accordance with the Lae Urban Development Study. This plan provides for the establishment of new industries, the opening up of new residential areas on to which the 'squatters' can be moved, and the creation of a green belt of parks and recreation areas along the Bumbu banks and the foreshore.[39] Not everyone has welcomed the emergence of the Ahi Association and one businessman in Lae has publicly condemned its members as 'irresponsible peoples'.[40] Despite such criticisms, however, the Association is performing an essential service for the village people. For the first time they have a legally constituted body which unites them and can act on their behalf in dealings with the government, the squatters, the local government councils, the mission, and the city business community; under its leadership the people have a strong chance of retaining their corporate identity and cohesiveness.

One scholar who has specialized in Melanesian studies has stated that Melanesian cultures have proved themselves to be adaptive and innovative. He believes that 'the impressive achievement of Melanesians is that they have developed authentic independent responses to the array of new experiences presented by European contact'.[41] This assessment applies above all to the Lae villagers. They have survived many disruptive changes. They narrowly escaped extermination in 1907–8 and after the cessation of tribal fighting and raiding they soon revived and their numbers were restored. They then endured the continuing onslaught of European settlement, the establishment of the town and the decay of their traditional society. After this they survived the Pacific War with its Japanese and Australian-American invasions. Finally they have seen the town grow into a city, which now encompasses and threatens to engulf them. If past experience is any guide, they will survive that too, possibly with the aid of the Ahi Association. Their society may perhaps be altered further, but they will remain a group that is conscious of the emotional and material bonds holding them together.

NOTES

1 *The Lae Before Contact with Europeans*

[1] For a discussion of the prehistoric migrations into New Guinea see J. Golson, 'Prehistory', *Encyclopaedia of Papua and New Guinea*, vol. 2, p. 961 ff.

[2] For a discussion of the differences between Austronesian and Non-Austronesian languages in New Guinea see A. Capell, 'Languages', *Encyclopaedia . . .* , vol. 2, p. 610 ff. For a discussion of the languages of the Morobe District see B. A. Hooley and K. McElhanon, *Languages of the Morobe District*. C. Schmitz, *Historische Probleme in Nordost-Neuguinea*.

[3] Schmitz, *Historische Probleme . . .* , p. 409 ff.

[4] H. I. Hogbin, *Transformation Scene: the changing culture of a New Guinea village*, p. 27, and 'Native Trade around the Huon Gulf, Northeast New Guinea', p. 244.

[5] Ibid.

[6] This myth was first published in a Yabem language primer for primary schools. It has been translated into English by the Revd K. Holzknecht, Lae and also appears in the Morobe Historical Society, *Journal*, vol. 1, no. 2, 1973, under the title 'Lo'wamung and Bombiyeng'.

[7] For a full discussion of social organization and leadership in Kawa society see H. I. Hogbin, *Kinship and Marriage in a New Guinea Village*.

[8] The state of 'primitive affluence' (affluence under conditions of subsistence agriculture) is discussed by E. K. Fisk, *New Guinea on the Threshold: aspects of social, political and economic development*, p. 23.

[9] For an account of lowlands subsistence agriculture in New Guinea see D. Howlett, *A Geography of Papua and New Guinea*, p. 51 ff.

[10] The trading system of the Huon Gulf is detailed in H. I. Hogbin, 'Native Trade around the Huon Gulf'; Morobe District canoe voyaging is discussed in T. G. Harding, *Voyagers of the Vitiaz Strait: a study of a New Guinea trade system*.

[11] These percentages have been determined by Hooley and McElhanon, see *Languages of the Morobe District*.

[12] Kawa marriage customs are discussed in H. I. Hogbin, 'Sex and Marriage in Busama, Northeast New Guinea', and *Kinship and Marriage in a New Guinea Village*.

[13] Ibid.

[14] Kawa spiritual beliefs are detailed in Hogbin, 'Pagan Religion in a New Guinea Village'.

[15] An account of the systems of Kawa magic is given in Hogbin, ibid.

[16] Details of the *Balum* cult beliefs and ceremonies are given in Hogbin, ibid.; Stephan Lehner, 'The Balum Cult of the Bukaua'; Schmitz, *Historische Probleme . . .* ; and Tibor Bodrogi, *Art in Northeast New Guinea*.

[17] Stephan Lehner, 'The Blood Theory of the Melanesians, New Guinea', details Kawa beliefs and rituals concerning blood and the related practice of cannibalism.

[18] Hogbin, 'Pagan Religion . . .', p. 130 ff.

[19] Ibid., p. 144.

2 The Arrival of the White Men

[1] J. Moresby, *Discoveries and Surveys in New Guinea and the D'Entrecasteaux Islands: A Cruise in Polynesia and Visits to the Pearl Shelling Stations in Torres Strait of H.M.S. Basilisk*, pp. 283-4.

[2] O. Finsch, 'Aus den Berichten des Dr. Finsch über die im Auftrage der Compagnie nach Neu Guinea ausgeführten Reisen', pp. 8-14.

[3] P. W. van der Veur, *Search for New Guinea's Boundaries: from Torres Strait to the Pacific*, pp. 14-20.

[4] O. Finsch, *Ethnologische Erfahrungen und Belegstücke aus der Südsee*.

[5] *Nachrichten über Kaiser-Wilhelms-land*, vol. 3, 1887, pp. 7-10; *Deutsche Kolonialzeitung*, vol. 4, 1887, pp. 108-10.

[6] *Nachrichten über Kaiser-Wilhelms-land*, vol. 3, 1887, pp. 164-7.

[7] Ibid.

[8] L. Kärnbach, 'Eine Bootsfahrt durch den Huon Golf in Kaiser Wilhelms-land', p. 172.

[9] Stuckhardt's comments come from a file of correspondence from the Madang District Office which survived the Australian occupation of Madang during World War I. The original file has now been lost, but a copy of Stuckhardt's report is held by the Land Titles Commission, Port Moresby.

[10] G. Souter, *New Guinea: the last unknown*, pp. 110-11.

[11] O. Fröhlich, 'Durch das Innere von Kaiser Wilhelmsland vom Huon Golf bis zur Astrolabe Bai', p. 201 ff.

[12] *Amtsblatt für das Schutzgebiet-Deutsch-Neuguinea*, 1909, pp. 135-7, 162.

[13] G. Heine, report to the New Guinea Company, Berlin, 8 Mar. 1911. English translation held by the Land Titles Commission, Port Moresby.

[14] R. Neuhauss, *Deutsch Neu-Guinea*, p. 44.

[15] J. Flierl, *Forty-Five Years in New Guinea: memories of the senior missionary*, p. 69.

[16] Fröhlich, op. cit., pp. 200-1.

[17] *Kirchliche Mitteilungen aus und über Nordamerika, Australien und Neu-Guinea*, vol. 40, no. 9, 1908, p. 68.

[18] *Kirchliche Mitteilungen . . .*, vol. 41, no. 12, 1909, p. 89.

[19] G. Pilhofer, *Die Geschichte der Neuendettelsauer Mission in Neuguinea*, vol. I, pp. 148-9.

[20] *Kirchliche Mitteilungen . . .*, vol. 40, no. 7, 1908, p. 51.

[21] Ibid., vol. 41, no. 12, 1909, p. 89.

[22] Pilhofer, op. cit., p. 149.

[23] *Kirchliche Mitteilungen . . .*, vol. 41, no. 12, 1909, p. 92.

[24] Ibid., vol. 42, no. 7, 1910, p. 52; and *Neuendettelsauer Missions-Blatt*, vol. I, no. 2, 1911, p. 9.

[25] *Neuendettelsauer Missions-Blatt*, vol. I, no. 2, 1911, p. 9.

[26] Ibid., p. 13.

[27] Ibid., p. 11.

[28] Ibid.

3 Early European Settlement

[1] J. A. Moses, 'The German Empire in Melanesia 1884-1914'.

[2] *Amtsblatt für das Schutzgebiet-Deutsch-Neuguinea*, 1912, pp. 5-7.

[3] G. Pilhofer, *Die Geschichte der Neuendettelsauer Mission in Neuguinea*, p. 149.

[4] C. D. Rowley, *The Australians in German New Guinea 1914-21*, pp. 101, 116; Moses, op. cit., p. 54.

[5] *Amtsblatt* . . . , 1913, pp. 79-81.

[6] The German Protectorate in the South Seas, *Official Annual Reports Published by the Imperial Colonial Office*, 1900-1, p. 3.

[7] Rowley, *The New Guinea Villager*, pp. 83-5; S. Epstein, 'The Tolai Big Man', pp. 44-6.

[8] *Kirchliche Mitteilungen aus und über Nordamerika, Australien und Neu-Guinea*, vol. 39, no. 9, 1907, p. 86.

[9] *Amtsblatt* . . . , 1912, p. 7.

[10] Rowley, *The Australians in German New Guinea 1914-21*, p. 101; Moses, op. cit., p. 54.

[11] *Amtsblatt* . . . , 1913, p. 80.

[12] Ibid.

[13] P. Sack, 'Land Law and Land Policy in German New Guinea', p. 111.

[14] *Amtsblatt* . . . , 1913, p. 80; *Deutsche Kolonialzeitung*, vol. 31, no. 15, 1914, p. 251.

[15] Ibid.

[16] Sack, op. cit., pp. 108-9; M. Jacobs, 'German New Guinea', p. 493; L. P. Mair, *Australia in New Guinea*, 1st ed., p. 93.

[17] Moses, op. cit., p. 54.

[18] *Amtsblatt* . . . , 1913, pp. 79-81.

[19] Mair, op. cit., pp. 178-80; Jacobs, op. cit., p. 493.

[20] *Amtsblatt* . . . , 1913, pp. 79-81.

[21] *Neuendettelsauer Missions-Blatt*, vol. 3, no. 7, 1913, p. 51.

[22] G. Schmutterer, 'Wogang: a chief among the Lae Christians'.

[23] Lae Mission Station, *Annual Reports*, 1911-21, p. 2. (Hereinafter abbreviated to L.M.S.A.R.)

[24] Hogbin noticed the same assimilation of old concepts by Christians at Busama, a Kawa village south of Lae. See his article, 'Native Christianity in a New Guinea Village', *Oceania*, vol. 18, no. 1, 1947-8.

[25] Schmutterer, 'Chronik der Station Lae', p. 2.

[26] *Neuendettelsauer Missions-Blatt*, vol. 13, no. 1/2, 1923, p. 4.

[27] L.M.S.A.R., July-Dec. 1925, p. 3.

[28] Ibid., 1911-21, p. 2.

[29] Ibid.

[30] Ibid., 1922, p. 2.

[31] Ibid., 1911-21, p. 2.

[32] Ibid.

[33] Ibid., p. 1.

[34] Ibid.

[35] Schmutterer, 'Chronik der Station Lae', p. 7.

[36] L.M.S.A.R., 1911-21, p. 1.

[37] *Neuendettelsauer Missions-Blatt*, vol. 11, no. 2, 1921, p 6.

[38] Ibid., vol. 13, no. 1/2, 1923, p. 4.

[39] Ibid., vol. 1, no. 2, 1911, p. 11.

[40] Ibid., vol. 3, no. 10, 1913, p. 74.

⁴¹ Ibid., vol. 15, no. 2, 1925, p. 13.
⁴² Ibid., vol. 13, no. 1/2, 1923, p. 4.
⁴³ L.M.S.A.R., 1926, pp. 1, 4.
⁴⁴ Flierl, *Forty-Five Years in New Guinea: memories of the senior missionary*, p. 104.
⁴⁵ *Neuendettelsauer Missions-Blatt*, vol. 14, no. 7, 1924, p. 36.
⁴⁶ Ibid.
⁴⁷ Schmutterer, 'Chronik der Station Lae', p. 6.

4 The Australians Enter Lae

¹ C. D. Rowley, *The Australians in German New Guinea 1914-21*, pp. 4-5.
² Ibid., p. 7. For the attitudes of the Lutheran missionaries, see G. Schmutterer, 'Chronik der Station Lae', for the war-time period.
³ Rowley, op. cit., p. 33.
⁴ M. Jacobs, *Encyclopaedia of Papua and New Guinea*, p. 517.
⁵ Ibid., pp. 492-4; J. A. Moses, 'The German Empire in Melanesia'; P. Biskup, 'Hermann Detzner: New Guinea's first coast watcher'.
⁶ Biskup, op. cit., pp. 13-14.
⁷ *Neuendettelsauer Missions-Blatt*, vol. 11, no. 11, 1921.
⁸ Rowley, op. cit., p. 42.
⁹ Ibid., p. 39.
¹⁰ Ibid., p. 246.
¹¹ Lieutenant E. E. Jones, 'Diary of Service as a District Officer in New Guinea' and 'Letterbook of Service as a District Officer in New Guinea'.
¹² Ibid., section headed 'Progress report Lae sub-station'.
¹³ Schmutterer, ibid., p. 12.
¹⁴ Jones, op. cit., letter to the District Officer, 23 Mar. 1919.
¹⁵ Ibid., letter to his wife, 20 April 1919.
¹⁶ Ibid., letter to the District Officer, 5 June 1919.
¹⁷ MS. Add. 122, 'Patrol Reports, Morobe', letters from Corporal Hickley to the District Officer, 6 Jan. and 6 Feb. 1918.
¹⁸ Schmutterer, 'Chronik der Station Lae', p. 10.
¹⁹ Rowley, op. cit., pp. 106-16; Mair, *Australia in New Guinea*, pp. 178-80.
²⁰ Australia, *Report to the League of Nations . . . September 1914 to June 1921*, p. 13.
²¹ J. Flierl, 'Co-operation by Lutheran Mission Finschhafen with the present government for the well-being of the aborigines of New Guinea', pp. 20-2.
²² Ibid., p. 6.
²³ Flierl, letter to the District Officer, Madang, 19 Oct. 1915; Australian Naval and Military Expeditionary Force, 'Miscellaneous Reports, December 1914-January 1916'.
²⁴ Flierl, 'Co-operation by Lutheran Mission Finschhafen . . . New Guinea', pp. 20-2.
²⁵ Ibid.
²⁶ Ibid., p. 24.
²⁷ Ibid., p. 36.
²⁸ Ibid.
²⁹ Ibid., p. 31. Flierl is here quoting a letter from the Administrator dated 21 Nov. 1918.
³⁰ Ibid., p. 36, quoting a letter from the Administrator dated 13 Mar. 1919.
³¹ E. E. Jones, op. cit., section headed 'Progress report Lae sub-station'.
³² Ibid.

[83] S. Lehner, 'Auszüge aus Chronikheft bzw. Stationstagebuch Kap Arkona', pp. 3-4.

[84] Ibid.

[85] MS. 199, 'Correspondence between the German Lutheran Missionaries and the British Authorities in the Mandated Territory of New Guinea; letter from the Morobe District Officer to the Administrator, 31 Aug. 1917.

[86] Ibid.

[87] Ibid.

[88] Jones, op. cit., letter to the District Officer, 28 Aug. 1919.

[89] Flierl, 'Co-operation by Lutheran Mission Finschhafen . . . New Guinea', p. 31.

[40] Ibid., p. 40.

[41] Lehner, op. cit., p. 5.

[42] Jones, op. cit., letter to the District Officer, 28 Aug. 1919.

[43] Lae Mission Station, *Annual Report*, (L.M.S.A.R.) 1925, (July-Dec.) pp. 3-4.

[44] Schmutterer, 'Chronik der Station Lae', p. 11.

[45] Ibid., p. 12.

[46] L.M.S.A.R., 1911-21, p. 2.

[47] Jones, op. cit., letter to the District Officer, 6 Sept. 1919.

[48] Ibid.

[49] Commonwealth of Australia, *Annual Report, Territory of New Guinea*, 1923-4, pp. 53-4.

[50] Ibid.

[51] Ibid., 1925-6, pp. 28-9.

[52] I. Grabowsky, 'A History in Diary Form of Civil Aviation in New Guinea', vol. 1, p. 72.

[53] L.M.S.A.R., 1925 (July-Dec.), pp. 3-4.

[54] L.M.S.A.R., 1936, p. 4.

5 *The Growth of a Town*

[1] The problems of transport between the coast and the goldfields have been described elsewhere. See A. M. Healy, *Bulolo: a history of the development of the Bulolo Region, New Guinea*; I. Grabowsky, 'A History in Diary Form of Civil Aviation in New Guinea'; F. Clune, *D'air devil: the story of 'Pard' Mustar, Australian air ace* (Sydney, 1941); I. Idriess, *Gold Dust and Ashes* (Sydney, 1964); L. Rhys, *Highlights and Flights in New Guinea* (London, 1942).

[2] A. M. Healy, ibid., p. 18.

[3] E. A. Mustar, 'Pilots of the Purple Twilight', *Rabaul Times*, 4 Oct. 1929.

[4] I. Grabowsky, ibid., Ch. 1.

[5] Ibid., pp. 145, 199.

[6] Territory of New Guinea, *New Guinea Gazette*, no. 180, 1927, p. 1239.

[7] Grabowsky, ibid., p. 59 ff.

[8] Ibid., p. 122; and Healey, ibid., pp. 46-8.

[9] Healy, ibid., pp. 45, 74.

[10] *Pacific Islands Monthly*, vol. 6, no. 3, 1935, p. 75.

[11] Ibid., vol. 6, no. 8, 1936, p. 47.

[12] Ibid., vol. 5, no. 12, 1935, p. 32.

[13] *Rabaul Times*, 20 Nov. 1936.

[14] Grabowsky, ibid., Ch. 1, p. 62; Ch. 7, p. 130.

[15] *Pacific Islands Monthly*, vol. 7, no. 7, 1937, pp. 8, 57.

[16] *Rabaul Times*, 24 Apr. 1936.

[17] Ibid.. 8 May 1936.

[18] Ibid., 19 Dec. 1930.
[19] Grabowsky, ibid., section for 1933, p. 171.
[20] *Rabaul Times*, 8 July 1932.
[21] Ibid., 14 Sept. 1934.
[22] Ibid.
[23] W. R. McNicoll, Private papers. See 'Future of Rabaul as the capital of the Territory', Cabinet agenda item 2244, 24 Nov. 1937.
[24] Griffiths Report, pp. 10-11.
[25] *Pacific Islands Monthly*, vol. 8, no. 12, 1938, p. 37.
[26] Ibid.; see also *Rabaul Times*, 1 July 1938 and 26 Sept. 1938.
[27] *Rabaul Times*, 21 Jan., 28 Jan., 1 July, 26 Aug., 9 Sept., 7 Oct. 1938.
[28] Ibid., 9 Sept. 1938.
[29] Ibid., 16 Dec. 1938.
[30] Eggleston Report, p. 47
[31] R. R. McNicoll, 'Sir Walter McNicoll as Administrator of the Mandated Territory', p. 122.
[32] Department of External Territories, Cabinet Paper No. 732, 3 Sept. 1941; W. R. McNicoll, Private papers.
[33] McNicoll, ibid., p. 122; *Pacific Islands Monthly*, vol. 12, no. 2, 1941, p. 63; A. J. Sweeting. 'Civilian wartime experience in the Territories of Papua and New Guinea', in P. Hasluck, *Australia In The War Of 1942–1945: the government and the people*, Canberra, 1970, p. 669.
[34] McNicoll, ibid., p. 122 ff.
[35] *Rabaul Times*, 21 Nov. 1941.
[36] W. R. McNicoll, letter to the government secretary, 27 Nov. 1941, W. R. McNicoll, Collected papers.
[37] Griffiths Report, pp. 10-11; Eggleston Report, p. 47.
[38] H. Nelson, *Papua New Guinea: black unity or black chaos?*, p. 23.
[39] *Pacific Islands Monthly*, vol. 12, no. 5, 1941, pp. 44-5.
[40] W. R. McNicoll, letter to the government secretary, 27 Nov. 1941, Collected papers.
[41] *Pacific Islands Monthly*, vol. 12, no. 7, 1942, pp. 34-5.

6 The Town, the Missionaries and the People

[1] Phillips Report, pp. 7-8.
[2] These statistics are drawn from the *Annual Report*, 1922-3 to 1928-9.
[3] *Annual Report*, to 1938-9.
[4] Lae Mission Station, *Annual Report*, (L.M.S.A.R.) 1926, p. 2.
[5] League of Nations, Permanent Mandates Commission, *Minutes*, vol. 15, 1929, p. 51.
[6] Ibid.
[7] Phillips Report, op. cit., pp. 9, 14, 157; see also Department of Home and Territories, 'Memorandum: report of committee of enquiry into native labour matters', Commonwealth Archives Office File No. AD 840/1/3.
[8] Permanent Mandates Commission, op. cit., vol. 15, pp. 49-51; vol. 18, p. 64; vol. 23, p. 27; vol. 24, pp. 176, 186; vol. 25, p. 47.
[9] Mair, *Australia in New Guinea*, 1st ed., pp. 151-2.
[10] L.M.S.A.R., 1930, p. 7.
[11] Ibid.
[12] Ibid., 1938, pp. 1-2.
[13] Ibid., 1936, p. 1.
[14] Gus O'Donnell, personal communication, 6 July 1971.
[15] L.M.S.A.R., 1938, p. 1.

[16] Ibid., 1932, p. 5.
[17] L. Malcolm, 'Marriage patterns, four Lae villages, pre- and post-1950'.
[18] L.M.S.A.R., 1935, p. 4.
[19] Ibid., 1938, p. 3.
[20] Ibid., 1935, p. 4.
[21] Ibid., 1934, pp. 4-5.
[22] Ibid., 1932, p. 4.
[23] Ibid., 1936, p. 4.
[24] Ibid., 1931, p. 2.
[25] Ibid., 1936, p. 2.
[26] Ibid., 1934, p. 4.
[27] Ibid., 1938, p. 2.
[28] Ibid., 1934, p. 4.
[29] Ibid., 1933, p. 4.
[30] E. K. Fisk, *New Guinea on the Threshold: aspects of social, political and economic development*, pp. 23-4.
[31] L.M.S.A.R., 1931, p. 3.
[32] Ibid.
[33] Ibid.
[34] Ibid., p. 4.
[35] Ibid., 1932, p. 1.
[36] Ibid., 1934, pp. 6-7.
[37] Ibid., 1938, p. 3.
[38] Ibid.
[39] Schmutterer, 'Chronik der Station Lae', section for 1933; see also L.M.S.A.R., 1933, p. 4.
[40] J. Flierl, *Observations and Experiences*, p. 21.
[41] L.M.S.A.R., 1936, p. 3.
[42] Ibid.
[43] Ibid., 1933, p. 7.
[44] Ibid.
[45] Ibid.
[46] Ibid.
[47] Ibid., 1936, p. 1.
[48] M. Boerner, 'My first term in New Guinea, 1931-40', pp. 8-9.
[49] *Rabaul Times*, 8 July, 1932.
[50] L.M.S.A.R., 1931, p. 5.
[51] Ibid., p. 3.
[52] Ibid., 1930, p. 6.
[53] Ibid., 1935, pp. 1-2.
[54] Ibid., 1937, p. 2.
[55] Ibid., 1926, p. 4.
[56] Ibid., 1938, p. 3.
[57] For a history of the villagers' land claim see I. Willis 'Lae's Land Grabbers'.
[58] Ibid., pp. 14-15.
[59] H. Nelson, *Papua New Guinea: black unity or black chaos?*, p. 223, has an interesting discussion on this point.
[60] *Rabaul Times*, 4 Oct. 1929.
[61] Nelson, op. cit., discusses this point.
[62] L.M.S.A.R., 1933, p. 4.
[63] Ibid.
[64] Ibid., 1930, pp. 5-6.
[65] Ibid., 1938, pp. 2-3.

7 War and Post-War

[1] N. Robinson, 'Butibam during the war'.
[2] N. Gejammec, 'Forty years' teaching in the Morobe District'.
[3] Ibid.
[4] I. Willis, 'Wakang and Kahata: *Luluais* of Lae'.
[5] Gejammec, op. cit.
[6] A. M. Maahs, *Our Eyes Were Opened*, Ch. 8.
[7] Gejammec, op. cit.
[8] T. P. Fricke, *We Found Them Waiting*, p. 24.
[9] G. Long, *Australia In The War Of 1939–1945: the final campaigns*, pp. 89–90.
[10] Lae Mission Station, *Annual Report*, 1946, p. 1.
[11] O. White, *Time Now, Time Before*, p. 8.
[12] *Pacific Islands Monthly*, vol. 17, no. 9, 1947, p. 30.
[13] Ibid.
[14] *Pacific Islands Monthly*, vol. 17, no. 4, 1946, p. 63.
[15] Ibid.
[16] Ibid.
[17] R. B. Rofe, 'Lae, New Guinea: An example of incipient urbanisation in a developing area', p. 5.
[18] Ibid.
[19] Ibid., p. 6.
[20] R. D. Taylor and Associates Pty Ltd, *Lae Urban Development Study*, p. 34.
[21] Ibid.
[22] Ibid.
[23] The figures quoted here supplied by Papua New Guinea Bureau of Census and Statistics.
[24] R. D. Taylor and Associates, op. cit., arrived at much lower figures, estimating that the population would reach 44 000 in 1975 and 100 000 in 1990. Their figures were based on the 1966 census and they did not have the 1971 census figures when they compiled their study.
[25] R. D. Taylor and Associates, op. cit., p. 135.
[26] Ibid., p. 77.
[27] Rofe, op. cit., p. 3.
[28] Ibid., p. 10.
[29] For a brief history of the introduction of urban local government in Lae see I. Willis and B. Adams, 'What's wrong with councils: the experiment at Lae'; see also B. Adams, 'The Lae Urban Local Government Council' and 'The Huon Council'.
[30] R. D. Taylor and Associates, op. cit., p. 221 ff.
[31] *Post-Courier* (Port Moresby), 19 Dec. 1972.
[32] R. D. Taylor and Associates, op. cit., p. 221 ff.
[33] I. Willis, 'Lae's Land Grabbers', p. 22.
[34] Ibid., p. 18; and also Willis, 'Wakang and Kahata: *Luluais* of Lae'.
[35] Ibid., p. 21.
[36] *Post-Courier*, 7 Mar. 1973, 9 Mar. 1973.
[37] *Post-Courier*, 28 Feb. 1973, 15 Mar. 1973.
[38] *Post-Courier*, 20 Mar. 1973, 13 Apr. 1973.
[39] *Post-Courier*, 22nd Mar. 1973, 27 Mar. 1973.
[40] *Lae Trading Post*, 18 Jan. 1973, p. 3.
[41] C. A. Valentine, 'Social and Cultural Change', *Encyclopaedia of Papua and New Guinea*, vol. 2, p. 1049.

BIBLIOGRAPHY OF WORKS CITED

PUBLISHED

Amtsblatt für das Schutzgebiet-Deutsch-Neuguinea, 1899-1914. Official gazette of the German New Guinea administration.

Annual Reports *see* Australia; 'Report to the League of Nations . . .'

Australia, *Report of the Committee Appointed to Investigate the New Site for the Administrative Head-Quarters of New Guinea*, 1938. Otherwise known as the Griffiths Report.

——, *Report of the Committee Appointed to Survey the Possibility of Establishing a Combined Administration of the Territories of Papua and New Guinea, and to Make a Recommendation as to a Capital Site*, in *Parliamentary Papers*, 1939. Otherwise known as the Eggleston Report.

——, *Report to the League of Nations on the Administration of the Territory of New Guinea*, 1922-23 to 1938-39. Otherwise known as the Annual Reports.

——, *Report to the League of Nations on the Administration of the Territory of New Guinea from September 1914 to June 1921*, Melbourne, 1922.

Biskup, P. 'Hermann Detzner: New Guinea's first coast watcher', *The Journal of the Papua New Guinea Society*, vol. 2, no. 1, 1968.

Bodrogi, T. *Art in Northeast New Guinea*. Budapest: Hungarian Academy of Sciences, 1961.

Capell, A. 'Languages', *Encyclopaedia of Papua and New Guinea*. Melbourne, 1972.

Deutsche Kolonialzeitung (Berlin), vol. 4, 1887; vol. 10, 1893; vol. 25, 1908; vol. 26, 1909. Newspaper containing information on the German colonies.

Deutsches Kolonialblatt (Berlin), vol. 19, 1908; vol. 22, 1911. An official journal dealing with the German protectorates.

'Eggleston Report' *see* Australia, 'Report of the Committee Appointed to Survey the Possibility of Establishing a Combined Administration . . .'

Epstein, S. 'The Tolai Big Man', *New Guinea and Australia, the Pacific and South-East Asia* (Sydney), vol. 7, no. 1, 1972.

Finsch, O. 'Aus den Berichten des Dr. Finsch über die im Auftrage der Compagnie nach Neu Guinea ausgeführten Reisen', *Nachrichten über Kaiser-Wilhelms-land*, vol. 1, 1885.

———, *Ethnologische Erfahrungen und Belegstücke aus der Südsee.* Vienna: A. Holzhausen, 1893.

Fisk, E. K. *New Guinea on the Threshold: aspects of social, political and economic development.* Canberra: Australian National University Press, 1966.

Flierl, J. *Forty-Five Years in New Guinea: memories of the senior missionary.* Chicago: Wartburg Publishing House, 1937.

———, *Observations and Experiences.* Tanunda, South Australia: Auricht, 1937.

Fricke, T. P. *We Found Them Waiting.* Columbus, Ohio: Wartburg Press, n. d.

Fröhlich, O. 'Durch das Innere von Kaiser Wilhelmsland vom Huon Golf bis zur Astrolabe Bai', *Mitteilungen aus den Deutschen Schutzgebiet mit Benutzungen Amtlichen Quellen*, vol. 21, 1908.

Gejammec, Nagong 'Forty years' teaching in the Morobe District'. Paper delivered to the Morobe District Historical Society, Lae, and subsequently published in the society's *Journal*, vol. 1, no. 1, 1973.

Golson, J. 'Prehistory', *Encyclopaedia of Papua and New Guinea.* Melbourne University Press, 1972.

Griffiths Report *see* Australia, 'Report of the Committee Appointed to Investigate the New Site . . .'

Harding, T. G. *Voyagers of the Vitiaz Strait: a study of a New Guinea trade system.* Seattle: University of Washington Press, 1967.

Healy, A. M. *Bulolo; a history of the development of the Bulolo Region, New Guinea*, New Guinea Research Unit Bulletin no. 15. Canberra: Australian National University Press, 1967.

Hogbin, H. I. 'Sex and Marriage in Busama, Northeast New Guinea', *Oceania*, vol. 17, no. 3, 1946.

———, 'Pagan Religion in a New Guinea Village', *Oceania*, vol. 18, no. 2, 1947.

———, 'Native Trade Around the Huon Gulf, Northeast New Guinea', Polynesian Society, *Journal*, vol. 5, no. 3, 1947.

———, *Transformation Scene: the changing culture of a New Guinea village.* London: Routledge and Kegan Paul, 1951.

———, *Kinship and Marriage in a New Guinea Village.* London: Athlone, 1963.

Hooley, B. A. and McElhanon, K. *Languages of the Morobe District*, Pacific Linguistic Studies, Series C, no. 13. Canberra: Australian National University, 1970.

Howlett, D. *A Geography of Papua and New Guinea.* Melbourne: Nelson, 1967.

Jacobs, M. 'German New Guinea', *Encyclopaedia of Papua and New Guinea.* Melbourne University Press, 1972.

Kärnbach, L. 'Eine Bootsfahrt durch den Huon Golf in Kaiser Wilhelmsland', *Deutsche Kolonialzeitung*, vol. 10, no. 13, 1893.

Kirchliche Mitteilungen aus und über Nordamerika, Australien und Neu-Guinea. Monthly newspaper serving as the official organ of the Neuendettelsau Mission Society, Bavaria, 1868-1910.

Lae Trading Post, 18 Jan. 1973. A Lae weekly advertiser.

Land Titles Commission, Port Moresby. Records relating to administration land at Lae.

League of Nations, Permanent Mandates Commission, *Minutes*, vol. 13, 1928; vol. 15, 1929; vol. 18, 1930; vol. 22, 1932; vol. 23, 1933; vol. 25, 1934; vol. 27, 1935; vol. 29, 1936; vol. 31, 1937; vol. 34, 1938; vol. 36, 1939.

Lehner, S. 'The Blood Theory of the Melanesians, New Guinea', Polynesian Society, *Journal*, vol. 37, 1928.

——, 'The Balum Cult of the Bukaua', *Oceania*, vol. 5, no. 3, 1934-5.

Long, G. *Australia In The War Of 1939-1945: the final campaigns*. Canberra: The Australian War Memorial, 1963.

Maahs, A. M. *Our Eyes Were Opened*. Columbus, Ohio: Wartburg Press, n. d.

Mair, L. P. *Australia in New Guinea*. London: Christopher's, 1948; Melbourne University Press, 1971.

McNicoll, R. R. 'Sir Walter McNicoll as Administrator of the Mandated Territory', *The History of Melanesia*. Canberra: Australian National University Press and the University of Papua and New Guinea, 1969.

Moresby, J. *Discoveries and Surveys in New Guinea and the D'Entrecasteaux Islands: a cruise in Polynesia and visits to the pearl shelling stations in Torres Strait of H.M.S. Basilisk*. London: John Murray, 1876.

Moses, J. A. 'The German Empire in Melanesia 1884-1914', *The History of Melanesia*. Canberra: Australian National University Press and the University of Papua and New Guinea, 1969.

Mustar, E. A. 'Pilots of the purple twilight', *Rabaul Times*, 4 Oct. 1929.

Nachrichten über Kaiser-Wilhelms-land (Berlin), vol. 3, 1887. Monthly newspaper of the Neu Guinea Compagnie.

Nelson, H. *Papua New Guinea: black unity or black chaos?* Melbourne: Penguin, 1972.

Neuendettelsauer Missions-Blatt, 1911-25. Monthly newspaper serving as the official organ of the Neuendettelsau Mission Society, Bavaria. (The successor to *Kirchliche Mitteilungen*.)

Neuhauss, R. *Deutsch Neu-Guinea*. Berlin: Reimer, 1911.

New Guinea Gazette, no. 180, 1927. Official government gazette.

Pacific Islands Monthly (Sydney), vol. 5 no. 12, vol. 6 no. 3, 1935; vol. 6 no. 8, 1936; vol. 7 no. 7, 1937; vol. 8 no. 12, 1938; vol. 12 nos 2 and 5, 1941; vol. 17 no. 4, 1946; and vol. 17 no. 9, 1947.

Papua New Guinea Post-Courier, 19 Dec. 1972; 18 Jan., 28 Feb., 7, 9, 15, 20, 22, 27 Mar., 13 Apr. 1973. Port Moresby daily newspaper.

Phillips Report *see* Territory of New Guinea, Committee of Enquiry under Mr Justice Phillips.

Pilhofer, G. *Die Geschichte der Neuendettelsauer Mission in Neuguinea*, Neuendettelsau, Bavaria: Freimund Verlag, 1964, vol. 1.

Rabaul Times, 19 Dec. 1930; 8 July 1932; 14 Sept. 1934; 24 Apr., 8 May, 20 Nov. 1936; 21, 28 Jan., 1 July, 26 Aug., 9 and 26 Sept., 7 Oct., 16 Dec. 1938; 21 Nov. 1941. Rabaul weekly newspaper published till 1942.

Rowley, C. D. *The Australians in German New Guinea 1914-1921*. Melbourne University Press, 1958.

———, *The New Guinea Villager*. Melbourne: Cheshire, 1965.

Sack, P. 'Land Law and Land Policy in German New Guinea', *The History of Melanesia*. Canberra: Australian National University Press and the University of Papua and New Guinea, 1969.

Schmitz, C. *Historische Probleme in Nordost-Neuguinea*. Wiesbaden: Franz Steiner, 1960.

Souter, G. *New Guinea: the last unknown*. Sydney: Angus & Robertson, 1963.

Supreme Court of Papua New Guinea, Appeal No. 139 of 1971 (N.G.). Otherwise known as the Butibam-Kamkunung Land Case.

Taylor, Russel D. and Associates Pty Ltd. *Lae Urban Development Study*. Papua New Guinea Department of Lands, Surveys and Mines, 1971.

Territory of New Guinea, Committee of Enquiry under Mr Justice Phillips appointed 6th Oct. 1927, *Report*, Rabaul, 1928. Otherwise known as the Phillips Report into Native Recruiting.

Valentine, C. A. 'Social and Cultural Change', *Encyclopaedia of Papua and New Guinea*. Melbourne University Press, 1972.

van der Veur, P. W. *Search for New Guinea's Boundaries: from Torres Strait to the Pacific*. Canberra: Australian National University Press, 1966.

White, O. *Time Now, Time Before*. Melbourne: Heinemann, 1967.

Willis, I. 'Lae's Land Grabbers', *New Guinea and Australia, the Pacific and South-East Asia*, vol. 6, no. 1, 1972.

——— and Adams B. 'What's wrong with councils: the experiment at Lae', *New Guinea and Australia, the Pacific and South-East Asia*, vol. 7, no. 3, 1972.

——— 'Wakang and Kahata: *Luluais* of Lae', J. Griffin (ed.), *They Came to New Guinea* [tentative title]. Canberra: Australian National University Press, publication forthcoming.

UNPUBLISHED

Adams, B. 'The Lae Urban Local Government Council' and 'The Huon Council'. Papers prepared as an M.A. sub-thesis, University of Papua New Guinea, 1973.

Australian Naval and Military Expeditionary Force, 'Miscellaneous Reports, December 1914–January 1916'. Australian War Memorial Library, Canberra.

Boerner, M. 'My first term in New Guinea, 1931-40'. Typescript of personal memoirs, n. d. Balob Teachers' College, Lae.

Butibam-Kamkunung Land Case *see* Appeal No. 139 of 1971.

File numbers AD 800/1/3, AB 824/1, AM 824/1, AD 840/1/3. Archives Office, Canberra.

Flierl, J. 'Co-operation by Lutheran Mission Finschhafen with the present government for the well-being of the aborigines of New Guinea'. Typescript report made to the Administrator, Rabaul, 1920.

Archives, Evangelical Lutheran Church of New Guinea, Ampo. Lae.

German Protectorate in the South Seas, 'Official Annual Reports Published by the Imperial Colonial Office', English translation of the German original by H. A. Thompson prepared for the Australian Administration of the Territory of New Guinea. Typescript, n. d. Library, University of Papua and New Guinea.

Grabowsky, I. 'A History in Diary Form of Civil Aviation in New Guinea'. Unpublished MS., n. d. Department of Civil Aviation, Melbourne; microfilm copy in the library, University of Papua New Guinea.

Jones, Lieutenant E. E. 'Diary of Service as a District Officer in New Guinea' and 'Letterbook of Service as a District Officer in New Guinea'. MSS bound in one volume, Mitchell Library, Sydney. These MSS give a vivid account of the duties patrol officers had to perform in the Lae region.

Lae Mission Station, Annual Reports. Typescript. Archives of the Evangelical Lutheran Church of New Guinea, Ampo, Lae.

Lehner, S. 'Auszüge aus Chronikheft bzw. Stationstagebuch Kap Arkona'. Typescript, n. d. Archives, Evangelical Lutheran Church of New Guinea, Ampo, Lae.

McNicoll, W. R. Collected papers. MS.2101, National Library, Canberra.
——, Private papers. Library, University of Papua New Guinea.

Malcolm, L. 'Marriage Patterns, four Lae villages pre- and post-1950', chart, produced for the Department of Public Health, n. d. Held by the author, Lae.

MS.199, 'Correspondence between the German Lutheran Missionaries and the British Authorities in the Mandated Territory of New Guinea'; and MS. Add. 122, 'Patrol Reports, Morobe', Dixson Library, Sydney.

Robinson, N. 'Butibam during the war'. (Paper delivered to the History Department seminar, 1972) University of Papua New Guinea.

Rofe, R. B. 'Lae, New Guinea: an example of incipient urbanisation in a developing area'. M.A. thesis. University of Wellington, New Zealand, 1967.

Schmutterer, G. 'Chronik der Station Lae', typescript, n. d. Archives, Evangelical Lutheran Congregation of New Guinea, Ampo, Lae.
——, 'Wogang: a chief among the Lae Christians', typescript, n.d. Mrs H. Holzknecht, Ampo, Lae.

INDEX